THE GIFT OF GRIEF AND LOSS

COURAGEOUS CARE

Dr Gunta Krumins-Caldwell

It's truly a privilege to share that I also have another book titled 'Puzzle Pieces of Life.' This book is more than just a collection of words; it's an invitation for readers to embark on a journey of self-discovery. Within its pages lie the keys to understanding aspects of themselves that may have previously remained elusive or misunderstood. By encouraging readers to reflect on the fragments of their existence that puzzle them, this book aims to unearth hidden truths and ignite a path towards self-awareness and liberation. It's my hope that through this exploration, readers will find clarity, fulfillment, and a renewed sense of purpose in their lives.

Ordering Information:

Prime Seven Media
518 Landmann St.
Tomah City, WI 54660

Printed in the United States of America

To my beautiful children-Seb and Lita
and their father Edgar

ACKNOWLEDGEMENTS

Everyone has a story to tell. No story is more important than the next, of this I am sure. Just that this story would not leave me alone and seemed to ask me to share it with the world. It was while Ed, my first husband, was still alive that the idea of writing this book began to germinate in my mind. Ed was the first to know that I felt it would be of value to write our story and was very supportive. So thank you Ed for acknowledging its worth.

I would like to acknowledge Basil Theophilous who so painstakingly typed my manuscript from my initial handwritten version. So many years ago, I felt far more at home handwriting than using a computer. It was Basil who could decipher my handwriting and begin to create a professional manuscript. I am indeed grateful for his patience and understanding.

Quietly, patiently and with his encouragement my second husband, Vivian, would read through my rough copies and make grammatical suggestions where he thought it was appropriate.

After Basil and Vivian comes a huge array of people that I call teachers our families, our friends, Erik Sandersen, my community, my patients, Ed's carers, and colleagues, the medical fraternity, the MND Care Foundation and anyone who touched our lives in those fragile years. All have been my mirrors from which I and my two beautiful children have learned. Without these teachers there would be no story and without them there would be no book.

We live emotionally fragile existences. This has always been so sharply illustrated to me in my day-to-day life-by my patients, laden with a bounty of stories. So many of them resonated with my own that it seemed inevitable that there needed to be a collective voice to these heart wrenching accounts.

I acknowledge all of my teachers and am indebted to each and every one of them, for they have made up the tapestry of my lessons. I would now like to share these lessons with the world and humbly help guide it toward a place of courageous care.

I would also like to thank Prime Seven Media for their guidance, expertise and support.

My two children Seb and Lit, have encouraged and supported me throughout this whole journey with love and respect. I could not ask for more.

And lastly, but most significantly, I acknowledge the Divine for guiding me and manifesting this book into print at the right time.

Thank you. Thank you. Thank you.

TABLE OF CONTENTS

WHO AM I?

————— ❧ —————

I am first and foremost a mother of two beautiful and exceptional souls, whom I have had the privilege of guiding through the first twenty-one and nineteen years of their lives. The four years leading to their father's death would have tried the most learned of people, but throughout these years, my children, aged six and eight when his decline began, shone with exceptional brightness. Notwithstanding the pain they experienced, they have never ceased to inspire and motivate me.

I have been working as a self-employed chiropractor and holistic health practitioner for thirty-three years. After having children, I worked part time and, in that time, I added a Post Graduate Diploma of Nutrition and, more recently, a Diploma of Spiritual Psychotherapy, and became a practitioner of Computerized Electrodermal Testing. I am a Certified NET (Neuro Emotional Technique) practitioner.

I have been working full time now for some twenty years and by the end of 2024 I will have been a registered chiropractor for 50 years.

I have worked solo in that time, as well as opening a multidisciplinary centre that I headed for 10 years. I have worked in other multidisciplinary centres and now again work solo with a colleague in a wellness centre.

My working life has been diverse, at times challenging but always enriching. Being able to combine a then part-time career (and now full-time) has given me a rich variety of perspectives on many life issues. In those four years, my work gave me a focus outside my own family problems.

I am passionate about helping people live better lives, be it physically, emotionally, or both. I feel a thrill when people are able to change their lives for the better because they take responsibility for themselves.

I feel passionate about life, but humbled by the journeys that people embark upon in their quest to live a richer life.

I feel fortunate to have experienced four years of extreme challenges on every imaginable level.

When my husband of twenty years was given a diagnosis with a prognosis of two to five years of living, I had to assess what I could do with such a life challenge. We were in the midst of bringing up two children, then aged six and eight years, and in the throes of a thriving business. I could live life by the moment and make the most of what was left of that part of my life or, as we chose, I could see what we, as a family and as individuals, could learn from such a life change.

We chose the *road less travelled* and therefore became confronted with all the challenges that would enable us to grow as individuals and as a family. That road was hard, rich, devastating, and full of realisations. We crumbled, we grew, and we crumbled again, until we realised that we had chosen a lifelong journey of self-realisation.

INTRODUCTION

———— ❧ ————

"This book is the product of what I have learned, achieved, and gained from being a mother, wife, carer, and counselor over four years as my husband was dying from motor neuron disease.

This book is about the myriad of lessons I learned. I have drawn upon the experiences of these lessons and used them as the source of my book. It is about what I have had to deal with, what my late husband had to deal with, and what my children had to go through.

Some of my experiences are not unique to someone living with a terminally ill person. Nevertheless, the way I dealt with issues, the depth with which I delved into these challenges and the painful realisations that I came to, I believe, have never been put together in a book, nor voiced in the public arena.

My book highlights one of my greatest lessons, and that is the lack of care and understanding for a family in our position in our society.

Our community needs this book because it addresses how each family member felt, how they reacted, and how they coped. It is not a story about what they each did, but about how, by being in their challenge, they learned to live and, as a result, grow from it.

There is a tragic lack of care in our society, both on a
professional level as well as on a personal level. Under
normal circumstances, it seems, we do not realize
how inept we are in dealing with terminal illness and
how deficient our society has become in care.

Out of the lack of care and understanding in our society came
the realisation that our society is afraid of death, afraid of all the
implications that that part of our journey asks of us. What do we do
with impending death, how do we deal with it, and how do we react
to it? Death is not an active part of our society's psyche. We do not
prepare for death, yet we must all experience it, both as observers and
as participants.

FOREWORD

My first encounter with this family occurred some two years after the diagnosis of motor neurone disease had been confirmed, and in the routine of my work. Armed with the cold facts of a referral, I was introduced, I explained the role I would play, and I discussed how this might assist to relieve the family of some of the physical burden of caring.

How little that referral prepared me for the spiritual and emotional burden carried by this family. What did I know of their lifestyle prior to diagnosis, and the profound change that they had undergone in every area of their life? The shattered hopes and dreams of a father who would not see his children reach maturity, of his wife who would be deprived of the joy of sharing the achievements of their children, and the children's sorrow that their father was no longer able to run and catch them in his arms. The family was dealing with the reality of these changes, as a unit, and each in his own individual way. Many hard decisions had been made, the well-being of the children being the paramount aim of the parents.

At this stage, Gunta and the children were managing Ed's care needs with very little outside assistance and with well-organised routines. It was not difficult in the course of conversation to assess where extra assistance may prove beneficial. But how does one ever assess the personal cost to a family faced at every turn with the life threatening disease of their husband and father. The demands on Gunta and the children to be carers left little time for their separate needs, or for their individual needs to be acknowledged as a partner or as a child in the very limited time left to them.

The ensuing months were a constant see-saw as Ed's needs rapidly increased, as options for care were tried, and either worked or failed, and new needs emerged. At a time when they needed privacy most, their home had to be open for the many people involved in providing care to Ed. The increased stress for Gunta was enormous and fraught with the inadequacies of a system unable to deal with the policies of meeting client needs when the going got tough.

As Ed deteriorated, the strain on the family became almost unbearable to watch, as the periods of respite in Caritas increased. Gunta remained strong in her resolve to care for Ed. She also remained strong in her role as a devoted mother, making some attempt to maintain normality in the lives of her children when their heads could make little sense of what was happening around them.

It is this sense of duty as a wife and mother and her strong conviction that others could learn from her experiences, whether physical, psychological, or spiritual, that has inspired Gunta to document so powerfully her account of a family devoted to the care and support of a husband and father diagnosed with a life threatening illness. It was my privilege to meet this family, to be accepted by them, and to walk with them for a short time along the way.

Terry Borg, Case Manager

"Death was never of God's fashioning; not for his pleasure does life cease to be; No end nor term is fixed to a life well lived."

-Wisdom 1:13, 15

ON SILVER WINGS

———————— ❧ ————————

The past it taught me well,
and sometimes though I fell,
the lessons were for me,
so let it be,
they came to set me free.

If God's plan for me is to reach high,
I accept the call, that's my desire
for within my heart, the everlasting dwells.

'Twas fate that showed me how
to profit in the now,
the game of life,
is stepping past the strife
so let us be,
it's come to set us free.

CHORUS
Let me voice my plea
and let me touch my destiny.
Fly me, fly me, on silver wings
to the place where angels sing.

Lyrics: Stuart Wilde
Vocal: Cecelia

CHAPTER 1

————— ⚜ —————

WEDNESDAY,
23RD SEPTEMBER, 1998

Guilt! Why doesn't it go away? It plagues me day and night. I feel boxed in! Everything I do seems to be wrong. I can't do anything as I would really like to and, in the end, I have to concede that I can only do what I think will best suit the children. They are my one constant source of inspiration. I am determined to create the best environment for them so that they can travel in the gentlest possible way along a very frightening and lonely road.

Here I am at the Royal Melbourne Show, putting on a brave face to give Sebi and Lita a day out of the ordinary, while their papa is in a hospice. Hopefully, he is being tended as I have instructed, within the bounds of their own code on how to deal with someone in the last stages of a horrible, terminal illness.

The mobile phone is on, attached to the belt on my jeans. I would not dare to put it in my handbag today and then not hear it ring.

Last night was terrible; yesterday was the worst! Taking Ed to the hospice last night took even longer than usual. I had prepared lots of new containers of different pureed soups and bottles of juice along with all the regular equipment and personal effects that would make Ed's stay at least reasonable, even though nothing really compared with being at home.

Ed struggled all day Tuesday. He had great difficulty swallowing and dealing with the mucous that kept filling up his mouth. He sat in his recliner for a while, then indicated that he needed to lie down. That took a lot of effort and care.

The recliner had to be raised for me to be able pull him to a standing position, and then I straddled him and carefully manoeuvred him to the office chair next to the recliner. Here was the shadow of a very tall, strongly built man with an imposing stature, reduced to a mere skeleton with only wasted remnants of muscles covering his long bones. He dribbled down his front and onto the floor, as he could not hold his mouth shut to contain his saliva and, even with the support collar, his head was flopped forward.

I manoeuvred Ed to his office chair and eased him into it. Then I raised his head partly and supported it by placing my hand over his forehead. There was a blank look, due to the muscle wastage, on his once-animated face. Ed's eyes, once sparkling and looking for attention, were focused on the task at hand. Was there still some fear of the road ahead? Oh, I'm sure there was! With my left hand supporting his head, I wheeled him around and pulled him backwards to the bedroom, where I pushed his chair against the bed, then steadied and braced myself. I gently yanked him to an upright position again, careful that, beforehand, I lowered his head. Ed shuffled the few steps to the side of the bed and, again bracing myself, I lowered him to the bed. I then held his head and lowered him to lie down and raised his legs onto the bed. Quickly, I turned him onto his side and positioned his hands so that they would be comfortable, so that Ed could breathe and could bring up mucous. Ed spat this out onto a towel on the pillow, and I wiped it away. Between these tasks, I would either sit staring blankly out the bedroom window, or, caressing Ed's forehead, I would whisper how much we loved him.

This Tuesday, it went on each time for a good half hour. Once he indicated an episode was over, the procedure to get him back to the study and into the recliner was in reverse order. It all took a good hour and then, within the hour, it had to be repeated.

God help me! I'm living in a capsule of tiredness, frustration, and helplessness a robot continuing my allotted tasks.

The day was exasperating, exhausting, and worrying. Ed had now reached the point where he could not be left on his own. He would need someone with him constantly. That would mean more rosters, more organisation, and more resources. Could this go on much longer? Not much sleep at night and trying to keep a household running during the day. Impossible. Every step felt impossible, but somehow I had to work it out and maintain a sense of equilibrium. Ed! Where are you, lost in a world reduced to physical struggles? Still stubborn, still demanding your needs, with barely enough muscle left to breath and swallow. Not at peace, just resigned to your ongoing journey, but at the same time looking for comfort and reassurance.

Where were the children? I had to feed them, feed Ed. I organised lunch, which we had in the study, with Ed in his recliner. Not much luck here. Ed couldn't cope with the way I tried to feed him. I seemed always to have difficulty holding the straw correctly in Ed's mouth so that he could suck up just enough fluid and then, hopefully, swallow it. I again had to lay him down. Trying to carry on a conversation in these circumstances really tested one's ability. But somehow I managed, and the children were now very used to their father choking, although their stomachs would churn with the sight before them, and the pain deep within them was hard to mask. I'm sure at times they found it hard to swallow their own food as a result of Ed's struggles. It was like swallowing down lumps of pain.

The day went on at a steady pace. In between attending to Ed, I packed his things and placed everything in the station wagon: clothes, books, toiletries, CDs, CD player, and page turner. There was no time to chat, no time to just sit and be there beside him. Each time, I was concerned that I would forget something. I organised for his electric wheelchair to be taken by taxi to the hospice, as the recliner would not be delivered until sometime on Wednesday.

Eventually, dinner time came, and the carer arrived to feed Ed. Again, Ed had the same problem. He couldn't eat, and with my help, the carer put him to bed to bring up the mucous. Now it was getting late. By the time I was able to get Ed into the car with the carer's help, it was coming on to eight PM. The children were getting tired and we still had a lot to do.

Sometime after eight PM, we arrived at the hospice. Then it was a matter of getting everything out of the car and setting it up in his room. The electric wheelchair had arrived, but it really wasn't as comfortable as the recliner. Nevertheless, we were able to get Ed into a manual wheelchair from the car and then, in his room and in the electric wheelchair. Sebi and Lita were exceptional, as always. They knew the routine by heart: what to do and how best to do it. After unpacking the car, we realised that we had forgotten the alphabet board that Ed needed to communicate. We decided that Sebi and Lita would stay and organise their papa and I would race home to get the board.

Careful, don't speed; concentrate on the road. It's too easy in my state of sleep deprivation not to be alert. This I managed, but by the time I arrived back, it was nine PM and all three of them were feeling frazzled. There was no means of communicating and, even though they tried so hard, it just led to frustrating misunderstandings.

Lita was getting angry with her Papa, and Sebi was just plain frustrated. They were two small children doing the tasks of adults, accepting what they had to do and mostly doing it, with a deep love for their papa. I say mostly, because, being so young, at times they just wanted to be children and forget about the pain that did not leave them. But their childhood had long gone, reappearing only occasionally as flashes.

Finally, after setting Ed up and giving instructions to the staff, we were able to leave, exhausted and unhappy, all three of us harbouring our own pain and shortcomings.

So, yes. Here I am at the show, watching the children go on some rides, going to various pavilions to see the animals, and then planning to watch the stunt cars in the main arena at three PM, just as the four of us had done a few short years ago. As we have some time to spare, we wander edinto a pavilion that has some products on sale. Suddenly, a lady sitting on a stool nudges me and says that I have missed a phone call, as the mobile phone screen says so. Funny, I didn't hear it ring, but the screen does say "1 call missed." The only call that is important is from the hospice. So I ring the hospice and ask if they have been trying to contact me. They check and answer no, but Ed has requested that we go in to visit him today. I ask them if there is a problem and am told there isn't, not to worry. Okay, then, I ask them to let Ed know we will be there, probably about five o'clock.

We watch the stunt cars, which the children really enjoy, and on the way out, they each purchase a fluffy puppet. Now it is time to hurry to catch the train home. We arrive home as the telephone is ringing; it is the hospice to say we had better hurry in. I reply that we are on our way. I tell the children to drop everything, we must hurry! I am focussed, but without any thoughts in my head. It is later than anticipated, just after five PM already.

On the way to the hospice, I telephone and ask the staff to let Ed know that we are only ten minutes away. There is a pause, and a voice at the other end says that she will get a nurse. One of Ed's attendant nurses answers, pauses, then says, "I'm sorry. Ed has just passed away." It is 5:20 PM.

CHAPTER 2

AMERICA

"If that is all there is to life
Then let's keep dancing
Bring out the booze
And have a ball."
-Peggy Lee

Where does one start to share a lifetime of experiences that seem to have been condensed into just three and half years of waking up and really living?

The years prior to May 1995 seem insignificant compared to what I have learned, experienced, and come to terms with in this short period of time. Although it was only four years, it seemed like an eternity of tears, heart ache, fatigue, and organising. Apart from the emotional trials that Ed and I experienced in our efforts to have children, my life previous to this seems now to have been a persistent lead-up to what I have learned since May 1995.

My life was not a fairytale before this, although it has been brought to my attention that many outsiders thought that it was. This irritated me so much!

Funny, isn't it, how people perceived this aura around us that life was just perfect and yet I never tried to create that impression.

Lucky! Funny, also, what people think luck is! A comfortable house, a good husband, a good job, perfect children, and, what's

6

more, a boy and girl in the right order, family, and friends. How everything always worked out so well for us!

Not only were we not a perfect family, there were many, many situations that indicated otherwise. There had always been ongoing battles with Ed's family, and these caused many strains in our marriage. Ed's family always found fault with me. I was never the right marriage partner, not being Catholic, for their golden boy. My family was too well off in comparison and my having an education left Ed's sisters feeling insecure around me, no matter to what lengths I went to, to be a part of their family. These issues led to questions of loyalties, and these created many disagreements over the years.

Perfectly lucky! On the surface, that's what it appeared to be and no one really pried or wanted to know otherwise. Materially, everything we had achieved up to this point was because of hard work. Everything emotionally, to maintain stability in our family, was also due to hard work, with many obstacles along the way. So why would onlookers pry below the surface? That may be dangerous! Flaws may become apparent and, worse still, it may become obvious that their own flaws are reflected, on closer scrutiny, into ours. We live such fragile existences, smoothing over constantly, never digging too deep, and never looking for the pain.

Yes, Ed was a successful cytogeneticist. He was also looked upon as the golden boy by his parents, particularly his father. Coming from a migrant working class family, Ed had achieved academic success. He found school easy, both academically and socially. Study was never hard, and he had an easy going manner that helped him become school captain at one of Geelong's leading schools, thereby giving him the opportunity to perfect his friendly and engaging nature. He had the ability to put people at ease, had empathy for the underdog, and could be the life of the party. Being the centre of attention was something he enjoyed, yet he never took advantage of this characteristic, although at times he had a tendency to overplay it. But then again, he had a commanding height at six foot three, was attractive, and had the manner of a knowledgeable man, so occasionally he would revel in this role.

Coming from a very strong Catholic upbringing, Ed had also embraced a religious perspective in his life. This was, at times, a hindrance in his ability to view certain aspects of life, but it also gave him a pivotal point from which he ventured very slowly along a slightly broader spiritual pathway. There was guilt, entwined with the pressure from his mother, as well as a very strong intellectual resistance to how I viewed conventional religion, particularly some aspects of the Roman Catholic Church. Over the years, we had many heated arguments related to religion and this led to arguments about his mother. Our separate beliefs in God were important to us and we both felt impelled to instil a Christian perspective into our children. There was a time in our journey, after Ed's diagnosis, where I felt our spiritual beliefs started to meld somewhat, but it was only temporary and, as time went on, our separate challenges illustrated the extent of the gulf between us in very subtle ways.

After graduating from Melbourne University with a Master's degree in Genetics, Ed worked for some years in the Genetics Department of the Royal Women's Hospital, eventually running the department. Throughout this period, he was involved in the Genetics Association as well as instigating improvement of methods used in prenatal diagnosis. He was highly regarded within his profession and eventually established the first private cytogenetics laboratory in Melbourne which went from strength to strength.

In February 1994, Ed had just completed negotiations with a large pathology service to form a partnership. So, there was cause for celebration. I was very proud of what Ed had achieved. He had worked extremely hard to reach this point, which had taken many years, and he had done it so well. The children, of course, were too young to understand any of this and we did not endeavour to explain it to them

Ed needed to travel again to the USA to meet up with colleagues and study the latest technology, as well as attend several conferences.

It so happened that straight after Ed's second conference there was a practitioner workshop I wanted to attend in Montana. Everything seemed to indicate that it would be a good opportunity for all of us to go to the States. We could make a holiday of the trip as well as catch up with friends in New York, and then spend a few days in Hawaii on the way back.

That was it, then! The children became very excited when we told them where we were going. This was no longer a plane trip to Queensland, but a very long plane trip to the other side of the world. We would be staying with friends in New York, going to San Diego Zoo, and staying at a dude ranch in Montana. We needed to organise passports and presents, but most importantly, we needed to determine if the hotels where we would be staying had a pool. For Lita and Sebi (five and seven, respectively), it was exciting, but they had to make sure the priorities were right. In other words, it really didn't matter where we were going, as long as we would all be together and had a pool to play around in!

Ed was due to fly out first to his conference and meetings, and the children and I would leave a week later. I felt that three weeks away from home for them would be plenty at their age.

The day arrived for papa to fly out and, even though we would be seeing him in a week's time, the children and I were already missing him. Lita and Sebi's favourite person wouldn't be there for them for the next week. There wouldn't be any door bell ringing at six PM to announce that papa was home, and there would be no stampede to the front door with kisses and hugs and lots of funny talk. There would be one less person to chase them around the house, play hide 'n' seek with them and, worst of all, they would be missing out on being put to bed by papa.

It was special when papa put them to bed because then Sebi and Lita would always convince Ed to make up a bedtime story, always different and always riveting. All three of them enjoyed these times immensely and now, with hindsight, I wish I had recorded them. So many memories could have been recorded but hindsight here is obsolete. Sadly, there are too few memories to reflect upon, too few to recall, to bring alive and share for the children's benefit, to clutch at and share with them. At least we have photos that prompt my memory. We should have taken more, but who thinks what the future will bring? Who knows what, in future years when we look back, will mean so much? Then again, maybe it is best to leave these times in the cloudy memory of childhood.

We survived our week by ourselves at home. There was plenty to do and think about besides work, and each day 1 explained something more to Sebi and Lita about the trip and where we would be going. By the time we arrived at the airport, they were well informed about the length of the trip and what was ahead of them.

The flight went smoothly, and Sebi and Lita behaved like seasoned international travellers, making the most of every mealtime and every activity, including sleep.

At L.A. Airport, they helped with the luggage and then, small as they were, they helped me get to the right part of the airport for our flight to San Diego. This short plane trip was also exciting as we flew in a twenty-seat plane, and the children laughed as Mama had to stoop in the plane to get to her seat!

We were met at the airport and taken to our hotel, which was also fun, because in order to get to our room, we needed to take a hotel buggy, as the hotel was spread over huge grounds. Ed's conference was here, but he was flying in later that day from Denver.

We had a few days to entertain ourselves. The children and I enjoyed the various sights of San Diego but, more importantly, the pool at the end of each day! Like most children, Sebi and Lita seized the moment and made the most of each situation. No jet lag, no time. Every night, to burn up excess energy, they would bounce and jump from one bed to the next, squealing with laughter, eyes alight and sparkling with the sheer contentedness of life. It was good to watch their joy of life.

All too soon we had to say goodbye to San Diego and travel to Montana, which people call God's country, and it is no wonder. From the spectacular scenery to the beautiful panoramic views, it was all breathtaking. The ice-capped mountains, the raging rivers, the still lakes left you in awe of the grandeur of nature. When we arrived at the Dude Ranch, it was 85°F (29°C) and, with a pool in view from our cabin, it was essential for us to check it out! So, after unpacking, having lunch, and taking a wander around the ranch, the children and I went swimming. Ed, unfortunately, had to go to a spouses' workshop, to learn the basics of muscle testing. My six-day workshop was for chiropractors and spouses, to clear their emotional issues via a technique called NET (Neuro Emotional Technique).

When we gathered for our first session together, we each had to stand up and explain briefly what we hoped to achieve over this six-day period for ourselves. I remember saying, when it was my turn, that I felt I was at a crossroads in my life. I felt I needed to make personal changes, and this technique seemed to be able to unlock the door to underlying issues, dramatically and quickly. It was only twelve months later that I recalled these thoughts and realised how significant they were. The issues that came up uncovered the door to the first few layers of my emotional blocks and, for Ed, the most enlightening aspect of the six days was that he was unable to trust himself or others.

On reflection, this workshop instigated my spiritual awakening. It propelled me forward along this path that, for the past fifteen years, I had been travelling very slowly. It was the beginning of being able to view life panoramically and with a depth that, although gradually developing, really hadn't expanded a great deal. It opened the door to looking at myself far more closely, as well as the people around me and, of course, it gave another dimension to my part-time chiropractic practice. To this day, I am not clear whether in the end there was much change in Ed's spiritual journey. Although Ed's beliefs had somewhat expanded past the restrictive Catholic dogma, he was nevertheless ruled by his intellect, and fear of what he couldn't grasp with his intellect left him emotionally paralysed within his religious upbringing.

I have always marvelled and been wholly in awe of my children, as I suppose any mother who is in love with her children will testify to. That does not mean I was not able to discipline them or guide them along their respective paths, but I have always felt that they have a depth of maturity and centeredness that belied their tender years.

This was evident when taking part in my chiropractic workshop. I had to organise a baby sitter for the children for the evening so that we could take part in a workshop. We were staying in cabins on the ranch and, as the evenings were cool, log fires were burning in the cabins. The log fires were in the front rooms of the cabins, behind which was the children's bedroom. I was concerned that they should not be left alone due to their age, as well as the risk of fire. But on this particular night, around eight PM, two faces appeared at the glass door of the conference centre, which was quite some distance from our cabin. My children were fully dressed and wanting us. I was obviously most surprised. When I asked them what they were doing out of bed, their reply was most definite! Their baby sitter thought that they were asleep and had gone out walking with her boyfriend. As they both knew that they shouldn't be left on their own, and definitely not wanting to fetch us in their pajamas, they had dressed and come looking for us! Needless to say, the baby sitter was told not to return!

The rest of the trip was spent with friends in New York, followed by a few days of sightseeing and boogie boarding in Hawaii. They were carefree days and we enjoyed the activities we had planned with the children. We were just being a family on holidays. Then it was home again, a return to work for both Ed and myself, and school and kinder for the children. Life again took on the normal rhythm with its ups and downs. At this stage, there was no indication that, twelve months later, our life would be turned upside down in so many ways and would never return to life as we knew it prior to May 1995.

CHAPTER 3

─────── ❧ ───────

SOMETIME IN JANUARY 1995

We live such shallow existences;
We skim the surface of life.
We marvel when we travel well
Along the surface of life.

Why would this year be any different from any other year? Each year brings minor variations, especially with children. This year, the children started new schools. Not being happy with the state system, we decided to send our children to private schools, even though it was earlier than we had anticipated. Lita was about to start year one and Sebi year three. I was very happy about changing schools, but Sebi, having a good group of mates, was loathe to leave his old school.

I suppose it was an evening like so many others when I would arrive home late from work. The children in bed, having been organised by Ed on another of these late evenings of mine, and we were in the kitchen talking about the day's events. Suddenly, Ed remarked that he had been having intermittent cramps, mainly in his upper arms, but also in his arms in general. He wondered what it could be and whether there was a possibility of a neck problem. It seemed feasible, as Ed spent many hours each day peering down his microscope, analysing slides. I probably adjusted his neck, although, thinking back, neither of us took much notice of these symptoms at this point, mainly because of their infrequency. We both regarded the symptoms as an occupational dilemma that regular treatment would keep at bay.

Life went on at a hectic pace as the children started their new schools. There was much to learn for all of us. It was particularly challenging for me, as most of the children's responsibilities fell onto my shoulders. Ed was busy with work; I could not expect him to help me to any great extent, though he was always willing to help when he could. There were new routines, new requirements, and new friends to make. Lita found it easy to settle in, or so it seemed at the time, but poor Sebi was finding it a struggle. He missed his old school mates and the new school was so much bigger, where far more was expected from each student. It was an intake year for Sebi, so at least he wasn't the only one who was new, but being a child who liked familiarity, this was a big challenge. It was only years later that I discovered how Lita struggled to fit into her new school but, at the time, she stoically did what was asked of her. No wonder anger started to rise in Lita's personality as she grappled with school and the impending scenario that was gradually building in her life.

Most of the first term and part of the second term were taken up with dealing with the children's new situations and counselling Sebi through his hard integration into his new school. But there were also many pleasant moments amongst the trials of life.

There were birthdays, Easter, and there was a camping holiday in the Grampians with friends from Melbourne and Adelaide. These were fun times, but busy times filled with anticipation and excitement, as we always seemed to want to pack so much into each week.

Whether it was visiting friends or having people over for dinner, there was always something going on. I was constantly juggling the different aspects of our life, being careful to fill in all appointments, responsibilities, and engagements in our kitchen calendar. It always looked so full, so hectic! How often I remarked that life just seemed to be going at such an incredibly intense pace that there was never any time for contemplation. Of course, it also felt as though one had meaning in one's life, that one was liked, that, by being busy, one's life was travelling well. Oh, how wrong we were, and how very soon we would find this out!

CHAPTER 4

———— ❧ ————

APRIL ALREADY

Life is good,
Life is fine,
Life is hard,
Life is predictable.

Was it late April, after Easter, Sebi's birthday and after the annual gathering with friends at the Grampians that life took on a sinister turn? Again, late one evening in the kitchen, as the day's events were being recounted, I noticed Ed's hands. particularly his left, did not look "right." On closer inspection, I observed that the muscles between his left thumb and index finger were markedly wasted and that the same muscles on his right hand were wasted, as well. I then asked Ed again about the arm cramps and was informed that they were still occurring, but infrequently. I exclaimed, why hadn't he mentioned the continuation of the cramps earlier? But Ed was not one to create a fuss about what he saw as an occupational symptom. I started asking him numerous questions about his arm movements and the ability to do his tasks. It seemed he was able to do all he needed to. It was at this point that I told Ed he needed to see our general practitioner to organise some tests to investigate these changes.

After moving to our present home nine years earlier, I had taken my time to find a GP that I felt I could relate to, who was in tune with my alternative approach to medicine. I had found Dr. Z to be good on a number of occasions and had developed a level of trust with him that felt comfortable. I suggested Ed visit him to see what needed to be done.

Dr. Z felt that he would like x-rays of Ed's neck as this seemed the most obvious place to start. These x-rays revealed nothing significant, and he felt there was no cause for concern. But, to be on the safe side, he would send Ed to Melbourne's top neurologist.

An appointment was made for a Wednesday in May at eight PM. I was to meet Ed at the professor's rooms, as he didn't see the point in coming home when work needed him. I arranged a baby sitter for the children well in advance. This appointment changed our lives forever. It was the defining point where I felt our lives could converge, but, as it eventually turned out, we were to be flung apart in an amazing sequence of events.

CHAPTER 5

———— ❧ ————

WEDNESDAY, 29TH MAY, AT EIGHT PM

There are battles to be fought
There are battles to be won
There are battles that can be fought
But only by one!

The professor took his time in taking down a history and listened carefully to what Ed and I had to say. I had asked several of my colleagues over the weeks leading up to this appointment what they felt could be the problem, but no one was able to make a suggestion. During those weeks, I had gradually started to feel a level of concern, but it was vague, somewhere in the background. I didn't feel the enormity of the wave that was about to come crashing down on us. Why would I? Our challenges were always relatively minor, everyday ones, not life changing ones. Other people seemed to have those, but not our families or friends. How narrowly we look at life, how infallible we think we all are.

About a week prior to this appointment, Ed was sitting next to Sebi in his bed, reading to him, when suddenly his lip visibly dropped and lost its shape. This lasted for several minutes before it regained its shape. I recounted this incident to the professor in amongst the many questions he asked Ed. The professor then made a physical examination by testing the contractibility of Ed's upper torso muscles. This was rather painful, as needles were inserted into his upper arms and upper back. Ed flinched several times, but otherwise looked ahead, patiently waiting for the procedure to end. The professor also asked us personal questions, such as how old our children were, what Ed's profession was, how his laboratory was established, and whether I was working. At the time, I thought the professor was being a caring practitioner, interested in his patients. Later I realised that these questions would normally have been out of place but for the diagnosis that he was about to give. Yet there I was, sitting in anticipation. Of what, I don't know, for my mind had blocked out everything except what was unfolding before my eyes. Sitting in some type of anticipation, like a child, not really grasping the enormity of the event and oblivious to what was about to take place, yet sensing the seriousness of the situation.

Then suddenly, the exam was over and Ed was dressed. The professor didn't mince his words, although he chose them carefully, rather caringly, and added that his in-room apparatus was not as accurate as his hospital equipment. He asked whether we knew of a condition called motor neurone disease (MND). Ed immediately replied, saying he did and that he had read the book by Stephen Hawking, famous not only for his book, but because he had survived MND for so many years. The professor nodded and said that that was his conclusion, given Ed's symptoms.

Life suddenly went into slow motion. I was hearing what was being said, but my mind was racing. Ed kept asking questions, including whether his particular form of MND could be genetic, meaning could Sebi be carrying the gene and what was the prognosis. The professor commented that he thought that it wasn't Kennedy's form. He also wanted Ed to have an MRI as there was a 1 percent chance that he could be wrong in his diagnosis.

Then I heard the professor say that his prognosis in Ed's case was between two to five years. Two to five years of life left! No! No way! This was not what was going to happen! The professor said we should put all our affairs in order and have that big trip we had always dreamt about. What big trip? What affairs in order? Why? Why would we do that? Why would we take this fairytale trip? To where? What would it achieve? Nothing! No. Other things needed to be done, far more important things than going to fairyland! Suddenly, in a flash I had become an adult. I was no longer a child with childish dreams.

I can still remember what I wore that night-strange what we remember! It seemed that every aspect of that night was etched in my mind till eternity. As we left, I had already built up a determination and a resolve that we would beat this! We would show everyone what could be done! People with cancer survived; well, why not MND?

It came as quite a shock to me some three years later when I found myself reflecting on this night and I realised that it was I who was determined to lick this condition. It was I who was about to start battle, and it was I who would be torn apart and put together again.

Having arrived in separate cars, we also went home separately, and that, too, was a projection of the future.

Arriving home, I thanked the baby-sitter then waited for Ed to arrive. We sat at the dining room table opposite one another, digesting the evening's events. I must say, it seemed like a blur of a myriad of thoughts, but the essence was that I knew exactly whom I was going to ring and what tack we had to take.

On reflection, maybe it was easier for me. I hadn't been given a death sentence. But no, it wasn't easy. I knew intuitively that it would have to be me who would set the pace of how we would handle every aspect of our new life. The enormity of the task at hand was only just starting to seep into my mind, dripping into my very being, and starting to shake my foundations. My whole life felt as though it had crumbled to rubble, and somehow I had to rebuild it: faster, better, and without the children being the wiser. There was no time to lose.

Ed said he needed time and space to come to terms with what he had been told. But wait. What are you feeling? What is going on in your head? Tell me, so I have something to hold on to something to clutch. I can't hold on to a void. I can't hold on to nothing. Please, I want to feel your pain, I want to feel your confusion, your desperation. I want to hold it, share it, to feel we belong to the same journey. But it was I who was feeling, and Ed who was blocking. I needed to share, to externalize, Ed needed to bury it deep within him and internalize it. Again, life went into slow motion. We went to bed, but not to sleep.

Through a fragmented sleep interspersed with an overwhelming sense of the magnitude of our challenge, my mind was bombarded with thoughts of how best to help Ed: emotionally, physically, spiritually. How would we achieve his healing, how would I protect the children, what would be the best approach, and whom should I ring first in pursuit of Ed's healing?

With the dawn came a type of reprieve. I could get up and move on with what I had to do. Another ordinary day! At least, that was exactly how it was going to be to the outside world.

CHAPTER 6

THE FOLLOWING DAYS

Once there was peace.
But was it peace?
Then came the storm.
But was it a storm?
Then came the eye
To steady my gaze.
Again came the storm
Followed truly by peace.

It must have been no later than five AM. I couldn't pretend to sleep anymore. The thought of staying in bed for one more moment became intolerable. There was a pervading numbness in my restless sleep, with a realisation of the magnitude of our challenge, punctuated by fear and disbelief. No tears yet. I felt washed out without much sleep, but that was pushed aside as the adrenalin started to pump, thinking about whom to ring first. Hopefully, the phoning would be done before the children woke up.

I also had to get ready for work. Another challenge. How was I going to do that? A full day of appointments and not one of them should become suspicious that suddenly my life was no longer as it had been yesterday. Did a steely strength manifest itself from deep within me? I suppose it must have, though at the time I seemed to be on automatic, dealing with what needed to be done. I wondered how

Ed was going to cope with his diagnosis, but he was good at masking his feelings. I wondered if he could do that now. For my part, it was all too raw. Numbness was still my best companion.

This was no ordinary illness that could be tackled in the normal, orthodox fashion. This was a horrendous illness, the ramifications of which, at this stage, I was not fully aware and was not about to find out, since this would take my focus away from how I was about to tackle everything. It would have left me wide open to all the negative aspects that, at this moment in time, were of no value.

If we were to reverse this illness, alternative healing methods needed to be investigated. I was only too aware that we were now in a vulnerable position. We could be tempted to chase every conceivable alternative method. I knew there could be no end to that, but I also knew that with nothing positive being offered by mainstream medicine, some forward alternative approaches would have to be explored, examined, and used.

Hence my impatience to ring the USA and speak to Scotty, the chiropractor who put together the technique called NET. Scotty was coming to Australia in June and July to present workshops and I needed to secure some of his precious time to see if we could come up with at least a few reasons for Ed's illness.

It must be realised that I was not coming from an orthodox approach. I did not believe that it was just plain bad luck that my husband had contracted this illness. It was not God bestowing his punishment upon us, and it certainly was not the devil getting the upper hand. Of all this, I was very sure, as was Ed. We are the masters of our destinies, the makers of our individual realities, and the creators of our separate worlds. It was my wakeup call, it was Ed's wakeup call, and it was the journey that all four of us had to make in our own individual ways. How that would evolve at this stage I had no idea, because first I had to tackle the practical aspects of what could be done.

Was Ed still asleep? I didn't know. I didn't want to disturb him, but wondered, as he knew what I was doing, how he could sleep or stay in bed. So many times, I would wonder at his passivity, his willingness to leave things as they were. How fear paralyses us, bringing us to our knees, immobilising our very being.

Taking a deep breath to steady my quivering body and racing heart, I rang Scotty. He became the first person to know of our plight. Amongst my deep sobs, my words to Scotty were incoherent. I kept hearing Scotty say to take a deep breath, relax, to take my time. All the while, I could feel these dangerous floodgates within me being forced open, as at the same time I was pushing them shut. Eventually, I was able to ask him whether he could spare some of his time while in Australia to see what he could discover with Ed about his illness. This was tentatively organised. Then it was a phone call to our local GP to tell him Ed's diagnosis and prognosis. Again, with a quivering voice and a body that could not stop shaking, I told him. Oh, how hard it was to steady my voice, how hard it was not to blubber. Dr Z was absolutely shocked with what I told him, no less so because he would have prided himself on at least having this illness in mind at the time of sending Ed off to the neurologist. But he did not, and this had a huge impact on him personally. I also, literally, begged him to see whether he could, through his contacts, make some suggestions of what we could try for Ed to help him. I anticipated him ringing me or Ed within a month or so, if for no other reason than just to see how we were coping. But this was not to be. As with many other people, this was all too daunting for him not just professionally because he had not suggested this diagnosis as a possibility, but also because he felt hopeless to offer any help. Wait, where did sympathy feature? The bottom line was, I couldn't give a damn if he wasn't able to personally come up with anything to suggest for Ed. All I wanted to hear was that he cared about us. I wanted him to extend himself in his capacity as a GP, to reach out and show us some empathy. I so desperately wanted someone to acknowledge the enormity of our life crisis. I wanted someone to give us some words of encouragement. Surely that wasn't a lot to ask, surely that was pretty simple, straightforward. I was reeling in disbelief, as if life was spinning me faster and faster, and not being able to catch anyone's eye to make contact, to feel their heart connect to mine. However, I learnt very quickly that he wasn't the only one who couldn't overcome his own shortcomings to extend a caring hand to us. Most of us can't.

So there I was, distraught and wrung out, after making two of the hardest phone calls I ever had to make. But all I had time for was to take several deep breaths and walk back into the household to deal with all the morning activities that needed to be tackled before taking my children to school.

It was as if I was in a daze, yet focused. I was now travelling on a different plane. This was no longer ordinary life, yet all around me life was going on as if nothing had changed. How could that be? How many times I would reflect on this over the next few years and how many times I would be astounded that all the small dramas and incidents that make up life just kept on happening, even though Ed and I were in the midst of a huge challenge. Wasn't that enough? Did God really want us to deal with everyday incidents as well? How come? Those little incidents would at times tip me over my emotional edge and I would succumb to deep sobs that wracked my body overwhelmingly as I grappled with the larger challenge. I was left drained and limp but strangely, with time, I learnt to roll with these life incidents and came to realise that the less I resisted, the better I was able to deal with them as well.

So Ed drove to work and, after taking the children to their schools, I went to work. That, too, was the hardest Thursday of my life. To remain focused, to give the impression that life was normal, took all my energy and yet, one of my friends, a patient of fifteen years, was astute enough to suggest I needed a hug. That made things even harder, with the grave possibility of breaking down completely. Teetering so close to the edge, it took all my willpower to regain my composure and just mention that Ed was not well. As the day wore on, it became somehow easier listening to other people's problems; it took the focus away from me, though every moment that I did have to myself, I kept thinking of the people I still had to ring in order to glean any information at all that would be of value to helping Ed.

By and by, the day finished as most Thursdays did, with me picking up the children from their schools, talking over the day's events while driving them home, and then leaving them with their nanny so I could go back to work. The children had only about two hours with their nanny, then Ed would arrive home to take over the evening's activities to have been for Ed to come home that evening, to be greeted by take over the evening's activities with them. How hard it must have been for Ed to come home that evening, to be greeted by two boisterous, loving children and not knowing what the future would hold.

We decided that evening that I would give up my position as chairperson of the Latvian School Parents Committee. Any other commitments would be cancelled so that we could concentrate on our family and what we were facing. The following evening with trepidation, and drawing on all my willpower, I rang the Latvian School principal, who was also a friend, to tell him that I could no longer continue in this role, only to be asked why. Not being ready to tell him the real reason, I blubbered out something about it not being a marriage problem that was behind this decision. After the telephone conversation, I felt a fool at how ineptly I had handled it and wondering what he must be thinking. So silly. As if it mattered at this moment in time.

Friday morning saw me taking the children to school as usual, and then driving to my parents to tell them the news. I kept hitting the steering wheel, my sight blurred by tears as I was driving, wondering why this was happening, yet knowing deep inside that this was how it was meant to be. Seeing the people in the streets getting on with their lives made me wonder why their lives had not changed, why everything seemed so normal. Why the reverberations from our life challenge somehow had not also changed theirs. Life seemed so normal on the outside, yet now I knew how wrong that could be.

It took me a while to explain the illness to my parents, the implications and the prognosis. I could see my mother wilting as she started to realise the full impact of the situation, and my father just kept saying that everything would be all right. I eventually left them with their thoughts to get on with my usual Friday shopping and errands and, before I could tell my sister, my mother had already told her. I felt strangely disappointed that I could not have been the one to tell her our news. There wasn't much to say after that.

A cloud of numbness seemed then to descend on my family. Numb, because they couldn't imagine anyone in their family being struck by something like this. Numb, because they, too, did not know what to do. Yet, here we all were, dealing with the news in our own individual ways that, with time, would become more and more stark.

One minute I would be coping with everyday life, the next there would be a sudden burst like a thunderclap deep within me and I would stagger to address the once-unimaginable that was fast becoming our real life. I felt I was being jerked backwards and forwards between two lives that were subtly, slowly blurring into one.

Ed had made some enquiries about meditation and decided to go to the Saturday morning session and learn how to meditate. That was a strange Saturday, like being in limbo, without the usual feeling of the start of a weekend, without the usual commitments, as we had decided not to take the children to Latvian school that day. It was a grey day, no sun; quiet and subdued as if the world was echoing somewhere in the distance, but we were no longer part of it. It was as if we were in our own capsule of grief and dismay, yet focussed and with a sense of background peace. It was like being in the eye of the storm. Having experienced part of the storm, we were now experiencing the false quiet-the eye. Even though we knew we would have to experience the other "role" of the storm, we did not know how intense it would be, or how long it would last.

When Ed arrived home from his meditation, he shared with me what he had learned, showing me and playing to me the meditation CD he had bought. This was our first introduction to meditation music and chants. It was a whole new world, one about which I knew only a little. This introduction to meditation was my first big step on the road to really learning about God, beginning to really understand God, and striving so hard to reach Him. Eventually, my meditations became my kick-start to the day, helping to unravel all that did not make sense and at the end of each day, it gave me space to quieten, to honour and to be with the only Being that would always have time for me, no matter how well or how badly I had dealt with that day. God walked me through some incredibly black days, some phenomenally hard journeys, some of which I hope I never have to go through again.

Ed was coming to terms with his diagnosis in so far as he could think about some of the things that were available to him to help him psychologically. Nevertheless, our meals were only partly eaten, and Ed kept to himself much of the time, not being able to relate to me emotionally. I was beginning to feel less and less able to deal with his withdrawal, as neither of us had anyone else to turn to. I felt devastated. Ed had spent most of his life in an emotional wilderness, resorting to his intellect to carry him along. Me, I needed to share, to explore my feelings, to understand them and to learn from them. It had been my own journey of self discovery that I had tried to share with Ed from the time we met. Now it was not to be.

Next came Sunday morning, when Ed had decided to go to Geelong to tell his mother. Ed's parents had divorced a year or so ago, and his father had moved to live in Latvia. I was taking the children to Sunday school and going to church myself. This would be the time to tell my pastor, with whom Ed and I had built up a good rapport over the past few years and who had become a friend as well. After church, we were invited to lunch with friends.

There we were, the three of us, standing at the entrance of our beautiful Lutheran Church. One has to see it to appreciate its beauty. Behind the altar is a two-storey glass wall into which has been mounted a huge wooden cross with an amber sun connecting the two parts of the cross, behind it, swaying in the breeze, can be seen a pine and eucalyptus tree, symbolic of the integration of the Latvian community within Australia.

What did I feel, as we walked in, holding hands, Sebi on one side and Lita on the other? I wanted to run, to run away, but it was as if someone was coaxing me gently, firmly, through the church door. As the three of us walked down the aisle, did my intuition whisper to me, ever so quietly, that one day we would again be walking hand in hand into this church, but for a very different reason? My faith and my sight were on the cross and it was along this path, steadfastly, that I had to lead my two beautiful children who, at this point, were totally oblivious, on a conscious level, to what was happening to their lives.

CHAPTER 7

───────── ❧ ─────────

FRAGMENTS

Fragments flung and strewn into space;
There are so many, but they are all me.
How do I retrieve them, put them together?
How do I know which piece goes where?
How do I survive in this fragmented world?

There I sat in church that Sunday morning, staring out to the beyond, past the cross, past the pine and eucalyptus tree, to the universe to which I was blind. I felt small, insignificant, and trembling within, devoid of the emotional tools to deal with our enormous trial. I only had an inkling of its brevity, its depth, and how it was beginning to overwhelm us, yet at the same time it was encapsulating us, squeezing us towards a path unknown.

Where were the answers, where was the road that I had to take? It was only my determination that was steering me at present, as I was blind, as yet, to my ordained path. The pain so deep, so very deep inside me, was like a fathomless, forgotten well from which came waves of deep, forgotten tears, the depth of which I only had a sense of as I prayed and listened to our pastor. I cannot remember what the sermon was about, but Aldis sermons always made me think, challenged me where I found myself and, no doubt, that is how it was that Sunday morning.

There I sat, after everyone had left, knowing Aldis would come to seek me out as he did anyone who remained in a pew after a service. He knew something was wrong as soon as he sat next to me. How could he not, with tears welling up in my eyes, lip determined not to tremble, yet not being immediately able to speak. Again, I needed to control myself, to steady my voice, to gulp back the flood of emotions. After telling Aldis and conveying my determination to beat this challenge, we prayed, holding hands. I was desperate to hold onto someone who tried to understand, someone like Aldis, who, through his congregation, had seen so much anguish. Aldis was there for me that morning as he was soon for both of us, to give of his time and his faith.

Unfortunately, this reassuring moment was over too soon, as we had arranged a time for the three of us to meet at our place for prayer and healing. Again, no matter how fragmented and ill at ease I felt, how heavy and inert deep within, I had to pull myself together to face my children and the world without them all knowing what was happening.

Sebi and Lita were eagerly waiting for me, as they were impatient to be off to our friends for lunch. They wanted to play with children they had known all their life.

A number of our friends were there, but all were tactful enough not to impose their curiosity onto me. I needed time to come to terms with my new life, my new perspective. So there I sat, socialising, (I'm sure very poorly) and so desperately apart. It was my first experience of becoming an awakened observer of life, not a partaker.

Later, as we arrived home, Ed was just returning from Geelong. Again, after the usual boisterous greeting that our children were so good at giving each of us, we were able to snatch a moment together, in the laundry, of all places. There, Ed related his time with his mother. He found it hard to recount this to me, tears welling up in his eyes, lips trembling. He stoically wanted to avoid breaking down, as he had found it so hard to tell his mother, no less so because Ed's mother is a harsh, uncompromising woman to whom life has dealt some very hard lessons. She was a big woman with an imposing demeanour and a countenance that rarely softened. So often she projected such heartlessness, saying that we all have our crosses to bear. On this occasion, however, she had cried and expressed that she would rather it was her than her son. Oh, how I wanted to hug him make it all better for him, but I couldn't; he wouldn't let me. Deep down, he couldn't allow me to get too close; the emotional turmoil was too great, the consequences too enormous. There was little I could do but watch, and hope the tears would eventually come so that we could both share each others desperation.

The next few days passed in a haze, interspersed with phone calls to several colleagues to ask for suggestions. One colleague, Richard in Queensland, felt he could be of assistance to Ed. He was not only a chiropractor, but qualified also in naturopathy, homeopathy, acupuncture, and NET. He had a large, successful practice, and he treated many conditions that mainstream medicine could not. Amongst his many successes, he had also treated a man diagnosed with MND. This man, he claimed, was a farmer who was now again working the land. After asking Richard many questions, I decided it would be worth seeing him while in Queensland attending Scotty's workshop.

The timing seemed to indicate that this was the right path. Everything was falling into place for our trip to Queensland. I felt encouraged and really excited that things appeared to be going as I had hoped. Ed was happy to comply, as he had not made any enquiries of his own; rather, he left it to me.

Although there were a few colleagues willing to help in whatever way possible, there were others, just like Dr Z, who did not return calls after I made personal contact with them and asked them to ring me back with whatever information they may have. Were these people, who saw only the futility of it all, and felt helpless to offer any professional advice, unable to put their professional egos aside to show their human side?

This was such a shock, such a rude awakening for me, as I could never imagine not returning a call like mine. These people seemed to be more concerned to keep their professional egos intact, rather than attempt to express their concern and care for us. Have we, as human beings, become so fragile that to show care equates to lack of professionalism? Do we really need to protect ourselves so vigorously, to keep our emotional doors so closed for fear of expressing ourselves, for fear people would see us as anything but perfect? Is it that, because this armour is so impenetrable, we have forgotten how to care?

At first, the word "care" reverberated through my mind rather subtly, but as time went on, it became like a hammer pounding my mind from every angle that did not subside for some years. Whether it was phone calls or whether it was lame excuses, with their owner's minds stuck in an emotionless, unsympathetic quagmire. Maybe the action of care could not raise itself above the owner's deep insecurities. Could it be that their fears created such a paralysis within that it gave them a beguiled, stunned look? In the midst of this realisation, I felt impotent to respond. My own pain was razor sharp. Withdrawing was safer; it left me feeling less vulnerable.

Life was becoming increasingly stark with each passing day and so Wednesday, 6th June, came racing to meet us ever so surreptitiously.

This second opinion was not really necessary, as we had no doubt that the professor's diagnosis was correct, but it served to rip our world further apart, to make sure we knew exactly what we faced. The neurologist performed a thorough, clinical examination, apologising for any discomfort he was causing, but without a flicker of emotion-oh, where was the expression of empathy explaining his findings as he went? The left side of Ed's body was weaker than his right, but the neurologist assured Ed that his legs were still strong! Still strong for what? Still strong for how long? What did it mean? Where did that leave Ed? With the examination eventually over, I sat listening to Ed's questions and the neurologist's answers. This time, Ed was not only asking pressing questions about the near future but also how, if he were to die, this could occur. These questions made my stomach churn. I felt nauseous, light headed, but it made me steel myself even more. This was not what I wanted to talk about at present. This was not what was on my immediate agenda! Dogmatic? No! Determined? Definitely!

At last, the consultation was over, and we were out of the room. It felt more like we were stumbling out, propelled by a diagnosis that confirmed our fate, then spat us out and into a lift on our way down to street level.

Another person was in the lift. Were they also living on borrowed time? Did they know how precious life was? Did they know what real life was all about? Did they know how important it was to live each moment, to cherish it, to embrace it? We stumbled into a nearby cafeteria and sat at a table holding hands. I kept reassuring Ed that we would fight this all the way and he reassured me that he did want to reverse this challenge. It was the only way I knew that made sense, even though I didn't feel reassured that Ed was so resolved.

Ed said he wanted to pay a visit to his high school days' priest who was now a priest of a diocese in Melbourne. This priest had christened Lita. I liked him. He was down to earth and pragmatic, a thinker, a man with a heart, a jovial, rotund man of Irish descent. On the one occasion that he met him, Sebi attempted to imitate Father's seated posture in a most hilarious way. I encouraged Ed to go, to share his crisis with someone he respected and who would truly listen.

Later, when Ed related to me how his time with Father had gone, I found it interesting that Ed's high school days" priest was relieved that it was Ed's health that brought him to him, rather than a marriage problem. Father thought the children would fare better with this situation than if it had been a protracted, traumatic, marriage breakdown. This was a surprising perspective to me, but no doubt based on many years of experience for him.

After Ed had left to visit Father and I had put the children to bed, I had this incredible urge to pray. It was an urge so deep, so wracked with grief, so pitiful, yet so submissive. The tears came from deep within as I knelt at the side of the bed, head in hands, focusing so hard on all that was happening and begging God's guidance with every fibre of my body.

There I was on my knees, probably not very long, for my journey to God was so new, when suddenly, clearly in my mind were the words, "Viss būs labi." (All will be well.) All will be well, all will be well! These words could not be mistaken. They were not my words; they were not my imagination. They were real. From then on, these words carried me forward for a good few years, until, suddenly, one day I realised that my initial understanding of these words was wrong, and yet the words and meaning remained true. How narrow our thought processes could be; how quick we are to see only one perspective and how quick to presume we know what is best for us!

CHAPTER 8

--- ❧ ---

LONELY

What do you hold onto
When you are lonely?
Where do you turn when
there is void all around?

Lonely. What is lonely? Does it mean lonely in a crowd; lonely being on one's own; lonely because we have argued with our best friend; lonely because someone does not understand what we are saying; lonely because we have nowhere to go this weekend? NO! NO! Those are transient times; we know we can take charge of them. We know tomorrow will be different. We know that for a short time we are alone, alone with our thoughts and maybe a time to reflect. No, loneliness is when you look all around you and there is nothing there! No signposts, no helping hand, no one to guide you.

The weeks following Ed's diagnosis were some of my blackest times, yet there were more to come. Until now, I had never experienced anything so black. The blackness was suffocating, all-consuming, all-pervading. It was with me day and night, constant and unrelenting. Being in a place I had never been before left me floundering, feeling for the boundaries in this blackness to which there seemed no end. This steeled me to tentatively move out of this blackness, no matter how hard and no matter how long it would take. I couldn't be consoled by my children; they were too young.

They needed me to be their strength. I wasn't able to be consoled by my family. They were struggling themselves, and did not know how to reach out to me and support me.

Where was I, where did I have to go, what did I have to do? Ed and I tried to seek solace in each other, but we only partly succeeded, not helped by the fact that, at this stage, there was no one else who could understand our misery and desperation. I needed to talk and talk. Ed tired of talking. He didn't feel there was any point in going over the same problem from different angles. He tried hard to pacify me, but I could not be pacified. I needed to hear what he was thinking, what his mind was doing, what he felt, what his fears were and how he was coping. I only gleaned inklings of his fears and thoughts. He just wanted to do what was at hand to deal with this challenge. He wasn't able to share his feelings, his anguish. Ed didn't want to be held or to confide his innermost feelings. They were kept battened down, even to himself.

I would sit crying on the edge of our bed, holding onto him, looking for some ray of light that would be of comfort, but there was none! Not because Ed wasn't there for me, but because, after a while, he became exasperated by my need to talk out every one of my feelings and fears. Whether it was the distant future or the immediate future, whether it was related to the children, money, or our changed life, I needed to express my fears and to hear Ed's response. I needed to hear between the lines what he was really saying, and none of this seemed to be very encouraging.

Even though Ed kept saying how determined he was and that he would beat the challenge, I could hear between these lines a quiet whisper that said he really didn't think he could. Was it the way he phrased his sentences or was it his body language, or both? The message they conveyed made me angry and frustrated. He had so much to live for, so many dreams that were still unfulfilled. Why would anyone want to opt out of a life such as his? I wanted to talk about these dreams, share our future, even if for just a while, just a little while.

I had started buying books that gave me insights into terminal illnesses, describing how people dealt with their changed circumstances. I read them avidly, gleaning any information I could that would be of help to Ed, looking for any scraps of inspiration. Amongst them, I found a story of a young woman with diagnosed MND who for six months sat in front of a mirror in her wheelchair and learned to love herself unconditionally by working through every issue of her life. At the end of six months, this lady got up out of her wheelchair and walked, healed by her own efforts. There were many stories, some much worse than ours. All of this material I gave to Ed to read, some of which he did and some of which he didn't. We would discuss the situations mentioned in these books and, all the while, I tried to encourage Ed to dig deeper within himself, to see what he could start to discover about himself.

All this was new ground to us. We really were amateurs in this life crisis, but this didn't deter me, didn't make me waver, because I knew I was learning, learning about a whole new aspect of life, learning about life as it really was. This was exciting. If I could have, I would have sat and read all day. I found the reading material uplifting and inspirational. My vision was expanding; I was peering over new horizons. If I happened to read something particularly relevant during the day, I would ring Ed to share it with him. My exhilaration at learning kept at bay my overwhelming loneliness with which, at this stage, I had no effective tools to deal. Yes, I was praying; yes, Ed was praying and meditating, but we were babies in this new arena. Oh, how much there was to learn.

During the day, it was easier to push this sticky, unrelenting, gnawing, uninhibited, indefatigable loneliness away. It was easier to immerse myself in the business of life: in my children, in my work, in Ed, and in the trivialities that make up life. At night, I pushed it away by reading, thinking, and discussing.

By doing all this, I thought I was crushing my loneliness, dealing with it, fighting it, conquering it. How wrong I was. It just kept hounding me. I felt hunted, for whichever way I turned, whatever I did, it was there in front of me. With time, I learned that nothing, but nothing, can be dealt with in this fashion. Unless you turn around and face it squarely, with courage and determination, nothing can be resolved, just deflected for a while. With ever-increasing persistence, whatever it is you have to face will come smashing back into your reality again, but with an ever-increasing force.

At this stage, all I could do was try to cope with my lonely state. This intense loneliness left me bereft of any sense of belonging. For the first time in my life, I started to comprehend the difference between loneliness and being alone. For many, many months I grappled with my loneliness in many excruciating ways. Standing amongst our friends, I felt separated, dejected in my unique battle. Walking through a shopping centre, I felt as if I was travelling in a capsule of pain and loneliness, with everyone skittering around me getting on with ordinary life. They all seemed to have such ordinary lives! When your own emotional pain is so intense, so blinding, there is no way of seeing another's. Eventually, through real praying and meditation, I emerged victorious over loneliness to live alone, knowing that to be alone is not lonely but a peaceful state of being that is exhilarating and liberating, allowing one's strength to flower.

CHAPTER 9

——————— ❧ ———————

GROWING AWARENESS

Where is God, but in our hearts,
Lying dormant, waiting patiently,
Waiting for the ego to surrender
So the waiting soul may flower.

I had been reading so much, digesting and absorbing everything I could. I discussed all my reading with Ed, sharing it all with him, and using him as a sounding board. Ed was good in this capacity; he helped me keep my feet on the ground, made me think through issues logically, not just ride with a new idea. But there were other times when he was plain tunnel-visioned, when a new idea about a particular issue didn't seem to have any impact on him. He just wouldn't look at it, probably because it was all too confronting. It would have required him to challenge himself, to see if it could be of relevance to him at times; this must have seemed too hard. It all appeared too nebulous, no facts, no certainty.

At the best of times, I would find this approach frustrating, but here, where we had to push the psychological boundaries as much as possible to see what we could achieve, what we could learn, it made me feel angry and worried. It made me angry because I just wanted Ed to look and explore and see where it would lead him and, if at the end of that process, he could honestly say he didn't agree with it, then I could have accepted it. But so many times he didn't! This then worried me and I could feel the panic rise inside me. I felt he wasn't prepared to stretch himself psychologically and, therefore, he really, deep, down was not ready to take the journey to heal himself.

I kept pushing, prompting, prodding, and encouraging, depending on what I felt was appropriate. My heart was ready to do anything and everything necessary, whatever it may be, but I felt we were operating from different perspectives: Ed, from a traditional scientific background, deeply coloured with his Catholic upbringing, and I came from an ill-defined Christian background, with my emphasis on always seeking an alternative, healthier approach to healing.

We struggled to find common ground to see the other's point of view and, admittedly, our general Christian view had found a narrow common road. It was this narrow common road that we had chiselled out that allowed Ed to see the benefit of my pastor coming to our house to pray for healing and to share our fears and aspirations. Aldis was one of the few people who at the time had the spiritual strength to respond to our need to talk and pray. I soon realized that emotional strength tends to be bland or inert, borne out of sheer willpower, whilst spiritual strength balanced with emotional awareness allows us to embrace whatever situation faces us.

Pastor Aldis is a man who many people call a fundamentalist, dogmatic Christian. What they perhaps fail to see is that he has a commitment to his beliefs and that requires of him the courage to challenge his own ability to be the Christian he aspires to be. Most people find this approach challenging and confronting. Maybe it disturbs their comfort zone of mediocrity and lack of discipline. Not that either Ed or I agreed with all of Aldis' beliefs. Aldis is a man of integrity, reasonably tall, slim, a man who seems to be purpose driven but, being the human being that he is at times he tends to put a foot wrong. People are apt to criticise him for this too quickly, for then perhaps they can live more comfortably in their soporific state of superficiality.

Aldis came on numerous occasions in the early days, sometimes with a church elder and sometimes on his own. We prayed, we cried, we listened as Aldis performed hands-on healing. I would be a pool of tears, so desperate to connect with God, so resolved to help. Occasionally, Ed would have tears in his eyes but more often, he would have a faraway look while he spoke in tongues. We were still in a dream-like state, that floating feeling we all know so well-just before we become fully awake in the morning, vaguely aware that morning has come. The rising realisation that we are fast approaching the need to get up, but not quite wanting to engage with the world as yet

We were certainly going through the right motions, but there wasn't the commitment there and certainly there wasn't the belief in any of us that healing would occur. Intellectually, we were all desperate for it to happen: it would be the proof we needed that God cared, that God had listened to us, that He had answered our prayers, that He wanted us to share this with the world. But, with each successive session, I became more and more aware that a lot more was required from all of us for this to occur. I came to realise that our belief was intellectual, not from the heart. Ed wanted the healing, but there was psychological work to be done for that to happen.

Eventually, the end of June arrived and we flew to Queensland for Ed to seek some emotional insights and for me to do my workshop. It was good to get away, yet hard. We left Sebi and Lita with my parents, knowing that they would be well looked after and that all four would enjoy their time together, but we would miss them. It was good to escape from everyday life for a few days, but this was no romantic weekend for two; this was a working weekend, and for Ed particularly.

While I was involved in my NET workshop, which is a powerful technique that can assess and alleviate the internal stressors that are creating barriers to our health and success, Ed was spending extensive time with various NET practitioners, peeling away the emotional layers to try and discover a key or keys as to why he may have this illness. After two days of exhaustive exploration and correction, it became obvious there were deep underlying issues, all layered one upon another. There was family, there was his work, and there was his perception of himself. There was a sense of subservience to his parents. I always felt that Ed had a blind loyalty to his parents and his sisters, one that he struggled with until the last year of his life, never really resolving it. Yes, he was the golden boy, and golden boys need to be perfect. It was a subtle, pervading message that had been given to him by his parents; as though the golden boy needed to merit his unique privileges. But surely perfection is a relative and oppressive state. We can try as hard as we like to please the other, but we are never too sure what that really is and so find ourselves in a dilemma where we have not pleased the party we so wished to. Far more importantly, we haven't honoured ourselves.

How often Ed ended up in arguments with his parents, particularly his mother, be it about religion, his view of life, or about me. Ed would not ring his parents just to avoid the next argument. Ed was the golden boy who ultimately did not have the right profession and did not marry the right woman. His lifestyle was a raw reminder to his parents of their lack of financial success. Ed also felt guilty about his parents' preferential treatment of him above his sisters. Intellectually, he could accept that ultimately, we choose our own success, but this he could not transform into a psychologically integrated acceptance. Ed's blind loyalty to his sisters was his way of appeasing this guilt from which he could not extricate himself, to the point that he would always listen to their criticism, be it about him or about me. Yes, he would argue against this criticism, but he never made the stand to permanently stop these arguments.

With this backdrop, how can any human being trust himself; how can we honour ourselves as worthwhile and worthy of walking God's earth?

During this same weekend, Ed also caught up with his sister, who generously inundated him with Christian books about healing and kept hounding him to read the Bible, where he would find all the answers. Ed also had time to scour a few bookshops for books that I and Aldis had recommended, and amongst his purchases was A Course in Miracles.

This book turned out to be more for me than for Ed, and was truly a blessing. It opened up my world to what I consider many miracles. It was the book that resonated so deeply within me that all my unanswered questions, all my acknowledged intuitions were at last made clearer. Not suddenly, and not in a single bang, but little by little each page uplifted me; each page took away another layer of opaqueness. I couldn't put it down, yet I did, to think through what I had just re-learnt. It was exciting. I wanted to sing, to dance, to become immersed in this knowledge. At last, I was awake - awake enough to begin my journey.

On our arrival home, *A Course in Miracles* became my reference book. What I couldn't understand in the Bible, I could in A Course in Miracles, which then made understanding of the Bible clearer. Certainly not everything, and not all at once, but gradually, my eyes started to open to God's love-that we have been created in love by God and that God yearns for us to respond to love. Our souls are not sinful; our egos are just off the mark, as Dr Scott Peck puts so well in his book, *The Road Less Travelled*. We create our fears, but we can just as well overcome them with perseverance and courage.

A strange time followed, as we continued to live in our capsule, building up the strength that we would need to tell our friends. We felt we had to consolidate our own new reality and live it before exposing ourselves to the outside world

Ed's hands were already becoming noticeably weaker. His fine motor ability in his fingers was reduced. He was starting to have trouble doing up his shirt buttons, but could still manage. I would help him; I would coax him and attempt to raise his spirits, always cajoling him to try and lift his mood, to keep fighting, to be positive. In hindsight, these words were as much for me as for Ed. The situation was terrifying, and I, too, needed encouragement.

Friends of ours were moving to Latvia to live. We invited them over with another four friends to say our good-byes and wish them well. By this stage, we were strong enough to mask our changed life circumstances and carry the night off in a frivolous spirit as we had many times before. The only indicator was Ed's fading ability to pour a glass of wine, as he several times hit the edge of the glass with the neck of the wine bottle as he poured. As everyone was boisterous and having a good time, it went unnoticed. Only I froze every time the incident occurred.

Suddenly, in our day-to-day activities, the trivia of life faded into a pool of insignificance. What was once important now meant nothing, what before seemed to happen to others, we were now living

What matter that a cake was slightly burnt; what matter that it was raining and the washing couldn't be brought in; what matter that one was tired and needed some sleep. Suddenly these were all just frivolous, every day details, details that meant nothing. They weren't life; they were just minor inconveniences that dominated such a huge part of our lives. Everyone around me seemed to complain about these trivialities, I had done so myself in the past.

Life. What is life? I asked myself. Life is seeing a child, grubby from playing with friends in a sandpit, and feeling the sheer joy of being. Life is splashing a loved one in the bath and feeling the tingle as the water hits the skin, or running your hand through your child's hair or your lover's and feeling goose bumps up your spine. Life is feeling one is accepted, loved for what you are, not for what they want you to be.

The distorted illusion that had seemed to be life was now brought sharply into focus, like the surface of a pond, distorted by ripples, becomes clearer once the ripples have ceased.

CHAPTER 10

—— ✿ ——

COINCIDENCES

Coincidence-what is it but
God's Grace
Humbling us into realising the
Vastness of God's Grace.

Coincidences have always fascinated me, and Ed seemed to have had many significant coincidences in his life, though none quite as telling as the one that came about in February 1995.

It was only after I began to read *A Course in Miracles* that those coincidences made sense. I had never regarded them as chances or fates, as people were apt to describe unusual occurrences; I felt that, good or bad, they happened for a reason.

Now I understood them as God's Grace, God's and our ability to orchestrate the most complex set of life circumstances to maximize our learning outcomes. As Scott Peck says, "God is efficient."

Ed was in the habit of frequenting the Victoria Market several times a week to buy a bratwurst and a cup of coffee for breakfast. He left for work early, so this was his treat! Ed was renowned amongst some of his friends for sourcing the best take-away places in town! Food was important to Ed; it served many roles in his life, from comforter to social mediator to an opportunity for sharing with friends and family.

It was one of these early mornings sometime in February that Ed struck up a conversation with a man who seemed to be a regular at the same stall as Ed. They appeared to be drawn to one another. Why? Only time revealed the reason.

This man's name is Moss. He had a twinkle in his eye and a smile on his lips that could not be mistaken, even through his greying beard. He also had a lively stride that seemed to slow a touch as his body ever-so-gradually succumbed to its own problems. At the time, he was chaplain of the Peter McCallum Hospital. He was involved in a meditation group comprising three other men. At first, Ed and Moss's meetings happened sporadically and without planning, but it was uncanny how many times they "happened" to meet. I felt that God was making sure their relationship was well established before June. June, by which time our life had been melted down and dramatically reconfigured.

After Ed was diagnosed with MND, he rang Moss at the hospital to arrange to meet with him. They decided to meet in the park opposite Ed's work, where privacy was guaranteed away from Ed's work environment.

God had introduced Ed to a man who was extremely familiar with terminal illness. Ultimately, it doesn't matter what the terminal illness is; the fear, the anger, the denial is the same. Ed was able to open up to a man who had seen all these emotions many times. The two men had been attracted to each other without consciously knowing it; both would gain immensely from their initial encounter, and only time would show how profound this would be.

Telling Moss helped Ed to familiarize himself with his new circumstances, helped him to verbalize how he now saw life. It was less confronting telling someone who had listened to many people after they had been diagnosed with a terminal illness. Ed gained solace and strength in this new relationship; this was a miracle.

Soon there came an invitation to join Moss's meditation group. The men met once a week to share the events of the week, to seek guidance from an inspirational text, and then meditate to music. Two of the other men in the group, Stuart and Pat, were Catholic priests and the third was the Managing Director at Peter McCallum who was not well. Sadly, he passed away at the end of 1995.

Ed had longed for Catholic company many times over the years but none had been satisfying, intellectually or emotionally. With Pat and Stuart, Ed found all his religious needs satisfied. Not only were they sharp intellectually, they were also thinking men who saw the limitations of their religion as well as the benefits. They were able to laugh at themselves and had a wicked sense of humour. Nothing was sacred when Stuart, Pat, and Moss were around!

Ed enjoyed the meditation sessions. He felt he belonged, and gained great comfort from these men, both individually and as a group. He was embraced, acknowledged, respected, and honoured as a man in his own right. Ed had missed out on strong male role models in his life and these men helped Ed's heart to expand in a masculine way that was new to him. Ed's ideas were challenged yet respected; he learned to grow in a loving and endearing group of men. There was neither judgment nor raw criticism.

Until the day Ed died, these meditation sessions were one of the highlights of his week. He looked forward to them with an ever-increasing need. But Ed was not the only one who gained from these men. Both Sebi and Lita looked forward to seeing all three men each week, as they always had the time and interest to have a meaningful conversation with them. These children felt embraced and understood in the most subtle of ways, yet it was not lost on them as they responded in like to these men in a warm and giving way.

Me, I was just deeply thankful to God for leading Ed to three men who embraced him in a way no one else ever had and seemed able to read my energy and act accordingly. Oh, how much our world needs to learn. How much fear stifles our ability to care, to reach out, and just be, to be in the presence of the unknown, the little understood, and accept that just being with someone in need is actually doing!

CHAPTER 11

————— ❧ —————

FRIENDS

Friends give when they feel they have nothing to give.
Friends accept when no one else will.

It was time to share. It was time to tell our friends how life had changed for us and how life would also change for them, or so I thought. Looking back, I was so naïve. I hadn't anticipated the range of reactions of other people's insecurities dressed up as respecting our privacy. My heart was broken, my mind was ever looking for answers, and all I had were my own skills of competency and a thirst to know, to rely on. Oh, how inadequate I felt. And my qualities, what were they? I had never really spent any time reflecting on what they could possibly be. Does anyone, until they are prompted by some life event.

I had this misguided concept that, even though it was our journey, it would be inevitable that our friends would be significantly affected, being in the slipstream of our life. Don't we all accommodate to our friends' changed circumstances, be it the birth of a child, a trip of a lifetime, or a change of a career? My rather arrogant presumption would soon prove wrong.

Maris, a tallish, stocky man with stark white blonde hair and a thick, well-trimmed beard tinged with orange-affable and easy going-had been Ed's friend for some thirty years and my friend all my life. We had weathered and supported each other through our life crises on many occasions, and he was the first friend we told. Maris and Ed were in the habit of catching up with each other fairly regularly over a lunchtime sandwich. Ed chose such a time to tell Maris his news. To say Maris was shocked would be a massive understatement

He wanted to know what the illness meant, as he had only fragmentary knowledge of it. Maris was in a daze after being given the news and was unable to ask Ed very much. There were tears, there were hugs, and then Maris left. He went home too distracted to work, too shocked and disturbed to sleep, and too concerned with what he could do to help to leave the situation as it was.

Sometime later, he told us both that he had already experienced another friend of his losing his wife a few years prior. After she had died, Maris resolved to be actively available as a friend if ever again he found himself in a similar situation. From that point on, Maris was someone we could always rely on.

Maris came back to Ed's work the next day in tears, desperate to know more about motor neurone disease and what he could do to help. Ed was touched by Maris' deep concern, as was I, and felt a compassion for where he found himself. I was moved to telephone Maris after Ed told me what had happened, to see if I could lighten the emotional load on him and to thank him for his concern. Maris was honest enough to say he was floundering in his ability to know what to do and how to help. His expression of care made me feel reassured that we could rely on him in whatever capacity he would be needed in the future. I felt relief, as if a barely perceptible fragment of a massive load had just been removed, relief that we would not be on our own.

I did not know how the future would unfold. I did not know what our needs as a family would be or what Ed's needs would be, but Maris lived up to his initial pledge so admirably and deeply, that Ed, especially, was truly blessed to have a friend such as Maris.

Maris's dedication to his friendship with Ed flourished; his care for his friend grew, and both men discovered what a friend really is.

Then there was Samantha, a Christian with whom I had been friends since the birth of our sons. As time passed, our families had become firm friends. It must have been no more than a week after telling Samantha the news that she arrived unannounced at my clinic to ask me to go and have a coffee. Perhaps Samantha had the courage to look at her own life, with all its deficiencies, to look at herself and to look within, for it takes courage to aspire to live up to the principles of the faith we attempt to follow. Maybe for this reason she found it easier than others to reach out and extend herself, as no one else seemed to be able to do.

Samantha began to come to our house on a weekly basis to pray, so all three of us could share our week. It was my first experience of praying aloud. Initially, it felt awkward but, with time, it became uplifting. We shared our fears, our disappointments, and our need to understand what our week meant to us in terms of what God was calling us to do. It was a momentary balm, to share, to be able to pour out our hearts to each other and know there would not be any criticism or derogatory remarks about what we were feeling or doing.

Samantha was fascinated with my need to expunge my ego of impatience. Impatience had always been a teacher for me, but never so strongly as when our children were born and I had to learn that, to be the mother I wanted to be, a measure of quiet understanding would go a long way in making my mothering far more enjoyable and positive. With Ed's illness, I had to learn, again, that an acknowledgement of my short comings was needed to bring about results as I watched my husband go about his healing as he wished to. That patience was also needed to surrender to God's will. I didn't realize when we started our weekly praying how tortuous and involved my lessons on patience would be, how hard letting go would be. These lessons would lead to deep transformations within me, with some very confronting realisations.

Not only was Samantha there weekly, but she was available to share my life's disappointments and frustrations at any time. It was at one of these weekly meetings that the three of us decided to start *A Course in Miracles* lessons. We felt that if the three of us were working our way through the lessons, we would always be more motivated and encourage each other to continue. These lessons really opened the door for me to understanding our material world in a different light. My perspective started to shift and my meditations became more focused.

Samantha, Ed, and I had some wonderful discussions and disagreements about A Course in Miracles, with Samantha coming from a strong Christian perspective, Ed from his Catholic background, dogmatic and fear based, and I came from somewhere out in left field, gradually finding my true spiritual calling. Samantha and I reflected many times how Ed was able to intellectually discuss whatever was at hand-his reasoning capacity was extremely sharp-but there was no involvement of his heart, his feelings. Ed's faith was built on facts that he had been taught. He knew his facts well, but what he felt seemed to elude him. The spark that ignites each of our lives was missing. Samantha had observed this well before his illness. There seemed to be deeper aspects of Ed's spirit that could not be reached, neither by himself nor by others. Men are often stifled from childhood and told not to cry. Be strong; be a man! Does that mean that men shouldn't have feelings, or that feelings are just for boys, but that these feelings should be beaten out of them as they get older? Why has our community taken such a wrong turn over so many centuries to see feelings as weak? I have always felt that to express ourselves takes courage. Surely saying what we feel is a sign of strength not weakness, and crying affords us the opportunity to express our vulnerability, opens our heart to the unknown, and gives us the chance to grow.

Again, I thought that, although we kept talking about healing and learning about how people could be healed differently, the conviction was missing. There was now a deepening commitment within our minds, but our hearts were flagging. I had read enough to realize that healing requires a deep conviction with the ability to pray from the depths of your soul. Paradoxically, our need to surrender to God's will thereby open one's heart to the voice of God.

It helps if this conviction is shared by a wider group of people who become involved in one person's healing journey. This wider conviction brings strength, reinforces what is possible, and creates a powerful energy that can catapult us along a miraculous path. This idea of a communal belief was my first encounter with how powerful the collective can be, how entrenched in our rigid belief systems we are, and how hard it is to rely on our own intuition to take us to a place where seemingly no one else has been. I so wanted company on this lonely journey, so wished for my intuition to be supported with outside props, but to no avail!

Maybe I was looking for excuses; maybe I was looking to lay blame elsewhere, but it seemed more than that. I felt we understood our need to intellectualize our beliefs, that we were going through the motions of living it but, as yet, we had to take the steps to internalize our knowledge. It did not help that all around us the mood seemed very sceptical, though in the end we have no one to chastise but ourselves for our lack of faith. My faith had to be accessed and brought up from the deep dark bowels of my being. No one could bring that about but me!

CHAPTER 12

TELLING OUR FRIENDS

Silence is such a lonely place.
It disconcerts our being.
We lose all our bearings.
We lose all hope.

The journey to tell our friends continued. That was a bleak and black journey in itself, let alone the realisations that followed - confusing and new!

It seemed to fall on my shoulders to tell most of our friends. Even though I found it hard, I hoped it would open up the emotional doors to building bridges in the future.

Each time I told a friend, I would brace myself and get ready for the emotional shock that would follow, get ready for the words to sink in, and for the realisation to dawn as to what I had just said. My whole body would be trembling; tears and emotions would percolate to the surface as I willed myself to hold back both. Please God, help me get through this ordeal yet again. Let me not succumb to being a blubbering mess. With some there were hugs, with others just a blank look and a touch of a hand. There is not much to say initially when someone delivers this type of news. It takes a while to realize the full implication of what becomes a complete life shift. After each encounter, I felt drained, as if I was floating in this surreal world, as if I had just delivered the most important speech of my life. I was encouraged after telling one friend when I arrived home the next day and found a beautiful bouquet of flowers waiting on our doorstep, with a simple card expressing her support for us as a family and how her family would like to help in whatever capacity they could. They are an unassuming family that find it hard to put words to feelings, but they were there on so many occasions in different ways, following through on their commitment as our friends. Oh yes, they found it hard, but they weren't prepared to shirk what they saw as their role as friends. To them, as to others, I am eternally grateful. Life would have been totally untenable without their support.

This solitary bouquet of flowers, with all the expressions voiced in the little card, brought grateful tears to my eyes. Apart from Maris and Samantha, this family was the only one there for us in the beginning. They were long-standing patients of mine who became unimposing but committed friends, following through what they had stated on their card. They were always ready to give me a hug, whisper an enquiry, and ask what they could do to help. None of these simple acts of care would take the pain away or ease the burden, but oh, how comforted I felt that someone cared enough to put their own daunting insecurities aside and reach out to us. It was like a balm, a momentary balm, building a bridge of care.

It was a bleak Sunday in July, with a cold wind blowing and grey skies. We had arranged to go on a picnic with another family. Ed had already started to feel the cold, particularly in his hands as the muscles were wasting away, but as yet not noticeably. With this in mind, I had purchased a pair of padded leather gloves to keep his hands warm. The children, as usual, were excited to be going on a picnic. They would be able to make a fire, toast marshmallows, and race around in the outdoors. At this stage, and for many months to come, they were oblivious to what was happening to their beloved papa.

Ed's finger dexterity was diminishing, so I had to pull the gloves onto his hands on arriving at our destination. Eating his meal outdoors was hard, as the gloves had to be removed and the cold made his wasting muscles stiff and less amenable to fine movements. I could see he felt awkward, still unused to hands that didn't quite do what was asked of them, finding it difficult to manoeuvre his knife and fork. All of this our friends saw; they had been told the day before. We even made a comment about Ed's hands, but still there was no response from them." Please, say something. "I thought to myself, don't make us do all the work, at least make it a bit easier for us to put our challenge into normal conversation. Help us, see where we are. We, too, are floundering to know the best way to deal with this. But nothing. Nothing at all. Oh, how hard it must have been for them!

With friends, I raised our battle more than once, only to be told that it was too confronting, their mortality too glaringly obvious, their lives too clearly finite. That was so sad to hear, but understandable. I even copied a section out of one of Dr Bernie Siegel's books, written by a woman whose husband was dying from cancer, which I hoped would help us communicate. I gave it to friends. Still there was deathly silence. No response, no reaching out. I wanted to share, to talk about how hard it was, how I didn't know where we were heading. It all felt so desperately sad.

There was no response from Ed's family, apart from his sister in Queensland who would ring to ask how his praying was going, how his Bible reading was going, and to tell us her opinion on what he needed to do to help himself.

With my own family, it was different. I was protective. I didn't want to make the load too big for them to bear. It was I who rang my parents daily. My mother who would always enquire how we were faring and I would only relate snippets, just to make sure they didn't feel left out. I tried to keep my own emotional trauma low key. I didn't feel I could burden them with the intricacies of my daily challenges. My mother's health was reasonable and I didn't want to upset her.

Nevertheless, I did expect more from my sister. I wanted her to reach out and feel my pain. Surely she could see how much I was hurting. Surely our endeavours to deal with our challenge were obvious, different from when I recounted how I was treated by Ed's family; the put downs, the criticisms, the contempt, none of which was acknowledged as anything more than fabrications or exaggerations on my part. But my relationship with my sister was too fragile, her own insecurities and mine too overwhelming for us to form a bridge. She would always be willing to help out by taking Sebi and Lita, as her two children and ours were good friends. This was my sister's way of showing her care and concern. We tended to swap if possible, and I would have her children over. I was always mindful of how much I imposed myself on my family. We were brought up to be independent, self-sufficient people. Reliance on others, even family, needed to be kept to a minimum.

But there were a few times when I literally screamed at her down the phone, wanting to force her to understand. It was probably an innocent comment, on her behalf, that felt like a lack of care. "Why," I screamed, hitting the kitchen bench top, "were people so overt in their congratulations and phone calls when our two children were born? My hospital room was packed with visitors most days after the children were born. I was inundated with presents, with phone calls, but now, now when there was nothing to celebrate, why was there nothing but silence?"

On reflection, being on such a high after the birth of both our long-awaited children, I could have done without all the flowers and the gifts. I longed to build bridges with these people who were overt with their congratulations then, so that we wouldn't feel so alone. Oh, how thankful I would have been.

The "lucky" family became an aberration to be avoided, to be talked about behind our backs, but never to our faces. The silence became deafening; my loneliness became acute. Yet with the few people who could share it, it became comforting. Better to be able to share with one who truly cared than with many blank faces.

CHAPTER 13

———— ❧ ————

PRAYER LEADS TO GOD

Pray. Do we ask?
Pray. Do we receive?
Pray. Do I know what is best for me?

It seems such a long, dark, tortuous, vague tunnel, starting in dim, distant childhood, when my yearning for God began.

I had always been eager to learn about God and Jesus and what they meant. I was fascinated by the simplified children's Bible stories, and would ask my parents to read them to me, over and over. I would peruse the accompanying pictures that were drawn so realistically, and become immersed in them, trying to imagine what it would be like to be living in those times and seeing Jesus in the flesh. As an eight-year-old, I begged my mother to buy me a picture of Jesus that I must have seen in a frequently passed religious shop. She finally relented and I had it hanging in my bedroom in such a way that I could always see it. I have it to this day, and now my daughter has it in her room.

I would ask questions about God and Jesus, just as children tend to do, but the answers never really satisfied me, yet I didn't pursue my curiosity, nor did anyone appear in my life as I was growing up who would help me along this path. Looking back, it was as if I was in a desert and had to find my own way. I prayed as best I knew how, asking either for God's guidance or for something more specific, but never really expecting an answer. My positive longing was ignited temporarily during my confirmation classes as a seventeen-year-old, although the best challenge of my faith came about when I met Ed. He had such a strong intellectual commitment to his Catholic faith but, to me, it seemed blindly bigoted. Nevertheless, the endless discussions and arguments we had certainly made me think, I realised how little I understood and how ill-equipped I was in any in-depth arguments with Ed.

As time went by, I learned ways to sharpen my reasoning in regard to my faith, and the arguments between Ed and me became more equally pitted. My discussions were based on my intuitive interpretation while Ed's came from his intellect and, as a result, our respective beliefs had not evolved much in the twenty years we had been together. Like most couples, we were distracted, busy building our material world, professionally, socially, and privately, and, though we read extensively, never quite in the direction of expanding our faith. The challenge of our children not coming along as we had planned certainly made me explore the possible reasons as to why. My reading became more oriented towards psychological elements that could be hindering my becoming pregnant, as there were no apparent physical reasons.

It was around this time that a "New Age" friend of ours who was always exploring avant-garde health frontiers introduced us to the book *Love Your Disease*, by John Harrison. As I read, it made such sense and starkly illustrated what I had been observing for years with patients, ourselves, and people around me. It brought home to me how profoundly we are influenced as children, how our emotional baggage accumulates and moulds lives so subtly, yet so completely. At around the same time, I was given the book *The Family Crucible*, by Whittaker and Napier. This book opened the door to my realisation of the extent that family dynamics play in a person's upbringing. It is written as a story and shows how each member of a family has a specific psychological role to play in order to maintain the family equilibrium.

Eventually, when our children did come along, active faith became more important. It was the time between the birth of Sebi and Lita that my church congregation gained a new pastor-Aldis amongst a huge uproar.

Both of these books and Aldis came knocking on my spiritual door ever so quietly, ever so gently. Even though the books were not at all spiritual in the true meaning of the word, they challenged the way I conducted myself in this world; they asked of me why I dealt with life as I did. This prompted me to start looking more closely at myself, getting to know more about me, and learning to explore more deeply those aspects that we all hide, even from ourselves.

It became starkly clear to both of us after the birth of Sebi that we had done nothing to resolve our religious differences and when both of us made it clear that we wanted to have Sebi christened within our own religions, huge disagreements began. The problem spilled over to our families. Everyone had a strong view as to where and how our children should be christened. Of course, Ed and I wanted so much to please our families as well as ourselves that it was quite impossible. These differences, between Ed and me, had all started long ago with our wedding and, till the day Ed died, there was a deep regret that we never had the opportunity to celebrate our marriage as we had dreamed and hoped.

Somehow in the end, we reached a resolution that satisfied neither family, but at the time we felt it was the best we could do. Sebi was christened at home by the then-Lutheran minister, and Lita was christened in our nearby Catholic church by Ed's former school priest, with our new Lutheran pastor presiding over the ceremony. How many disagreements occur in this world of ours in the name of religion? How sad that everyone feels that their religion is the chosen one, each religion vying for its supremacy. Where is the tolerance, where is the unconditional care for our fellow being? We seem to live in a fragmented world, wanting confirmation of our fragile credibility.

When we both again tackled this dilemma after Lita's birth, we invited Father to discuss the matter. As soon as this big, man entered our house, there descended a sense of peace. Sebi must also have felt this peace and was drawn to it. He immediately took a liking to this man and attempted to mimic his sitting posture. There Father sat, cross-legged in the middle of one of our long couches, arms outstretched, resting over the back of the couch. On another couch, opposite, sat twenty-one- month-old Sebi, cross-legged, with arms stretched straight, trying unsuccessfully to get his hands to even reach the top of the couch! What a funny, precious memory!

Father brought with him his wisdom from years of experience. His words were reassuring; he explained that any deep commitment to a sacrament did not need any action to acknowledge it. Deep, true intent was all that was necessary in the eyes of God. Up to that point, no words of faith had ever rung so true as these. I felt that these words did not belong to any one religion; they belonged to a commitment and faith in God. How vindicated I felt then, when Father recounted his telephone confrontation with Ed's mother, who was suspicious of how Father would conduct his christening of Lita. When they talked, she needlessly attacked him, saying "You are not fit to be a priest!" Father was calm and considerate in his response to her vitriolic tirade, saying that all she needed to do was to actively love her son and his family-nothing else mattered. I knew that this was too difficult for her to hear; so sad that her anger about how she saw her religion was so deep, so intractable.

Life takes us along a convoluted journey, but the journey becomes irrelevant if, along the way, we don't begin to discover the essence of life: Love. That is such a demanding emotion that we are rarely privy to its magnificence and its magnitude. Our fragile egos are good at masking it in so many guises. We buy things for our loved ones, because we "love" them. We deny ourselves things because we "love." We extend ourselves because we "love." We keep going because we "love." But do we? Do we really live love? These are all actions that create the impression that we love, but how many times are they carried out with only responsibility, guilt, fear, low self-esteem, or anger as the motivator? Then, when we are not recognised for what we have done, we think we are not loved! Love requires justification; it just is!

We pray for love, but how do we "acquire" love if we don't love ourselves first, if we don't accept God's love? Love is demanding of us; it requires us to look within and, above all we surely evolve. With this can come a deeper understanding of self and, therefore, hopefully, of others. This requires surrender to where we are and surrender to transformation. Succumbing to life's lessons, with all the challenges that they bring, can truly lead to change, revealing some raw truth about who we are and how to see the world around us. What is best for us is not always pleasurable, not always immediately understood, but if looked at closely, necessary for our growth. So I prayed and waited for God's next lesson

CHAPTER 14

I NEED A HUG

I need a hug,
At all the wrong times
To share my pain,
To feel another human being,
When no one is around;
From you who cannot give me one
When I don't feel so vulnerable
Though yesterday I told you I couldn't.
But, no one gives that kind of hug.

Honesty and truth have always been crucial to me, and to Ed. Many a time we argued about the true essence of these words. By applying our own distorted meaning, we justify our perception of honesty and truth. Justification appears such a grubby word to hide behind. It lacks courage and substance, yet we often hide behind it. We can try to rationalize away everything in our lives by justification. It may be the way we react to someone's rudeness or to someone's joy. We all have preconceived ideas. Could it be we project these as a means of acknowledging ourselves, rather than having the courage to accept another's response? It is so easy to do and it makes such good sense, but where does it leave us? We are left on the surface of life, perhaps floundering to stay afloat where we wont have to dip below our emotional murky waters and ask of ourselves why such justification maybe necessary.

Could it be that honesty requires us to look at ourselves first to see the truth about what we don't like about ourselves and what it is we would rather not see? If we don't see it, we won't have to change it! That's convenient! So safe! Why disturb the surface of life when we can sail across it without a ripple! Oh yes, it makes for easy relations, it makes for pleasantries, but it struck me that it is so shallow.

To keep diving below the surface and view the emotional murkiness requires perseverance, fortitude, and the strength to suffer the consequences of what we may find. Why would we want to do that? The only answer to that can be self-growth. It brings out our ugliness. It requires us to take off our rose- coloured glasses and observe our surroundings unadorned. This can be frightening and paralysing for, all of a sudden, our life is not what it seemed.

However, the pursuit of self-growth can lead to honesty about ourselves and others. Who are we, what do we project, and what do we own? Honesty is multi-layered, depending on how truthful we can be with ourselves, as well as with others. Eventually, honesty can lead to truth. Are we caring to one another and to ourselves? Do we have the courage to reach out and share our vulnerability, show that we want to care, not by actions, not by words, but just by being? By being Love. Can we be Love, even just for a moment, every now and then, and not be afraid to receive as well as to give? If we can, that is a rich experience!

We lead such anonymous lives, living in our obscurity racing around, finding purpose, justifying our existence. We have become islands-islands at sea-bobbing up and down like flotsam that becomes fragmented as it floats. More and more we are losing our sense of community, despite many of us trying hard to belong to one. Finding a commonality-whether it be ethnic background, life circumstances, or common interests may give us a sense of belonging, but this is soon tested, as Ed and I found, when there is a serious life change.

Our life fell into a new rhythm. Ed's physical symptoms were quite subtle at this point. So, on the surface, our life appeared quite normal, except for a few minor changes. We were praying and meditating daily, Samantha and Aldis dropped by independently for some prayer time, and instead of discussing the daily news, Ed and I would spend time discussing our spiritual readings.

Often, however, I would suddenly feel as though I had unknowingly let go of these life ropes, as though I was drowning or being swamped by huge waves of water that I would try and gulp in or rise above. I would feel this blackness descend over me. I would feel overwhelmed by the enormity of what I was trying to achieve, by what Ed was trying to conquer, and I would be a sea of tears, inconsolable, wracked by emotions that would come pouring out of me. I would need a release for my frustrations, my shortcomings, Ed's shortcomings, and my constant disappointment about our slow progress, my fear about what the future held. Inevitably, it would be one of these times when I would get the rare telephone call from a family member or a friend, and I would be incapable of talking to them. I tried to say as much but, unfortunately, they seemed to be so frightened by my sense of not coping at that moment that it created an unfortunate awkwardness. Maybe this was the reason why they did not have the courage to call me back in a day or so.

I would hope for a return call, but it would never be. Once, I found flowers on my doorstep from a well-meaning friend, but still no physical contact. On the few occasions that I ventured into sharing my feelings or thoughts, I was either looked upon blankly or I would receive a justification as to why people are as they are.

I wanted people to reach out. I was beginning to find it too hard. I felt I was withdrawing, withdrawing into my awful, painful shell. At least that was tangible, that was faithful, ever constant. Yes, we felt that people had let us down, although later …. much later, it crossed my mind that the only people who let us down were ourselves for having too many high and unrealistic expectations.

We have daydreams that our friends will be there in the bad times just as they are in the good times, but how do we know? We only presume. Presumption is a dangerous projection, for it asks that which has never been tested, and we are devastated when people fail our test.

Gestures: what do they mean? It is true that some gestures leave us feeling warm inside, however some seem to be rather neutral and others can make us cringe, for we know intuitively, that they are not genuine, just a token. The gestures that came our way were as varied as the people. So it must be, for we are all individuals with our own way of expressing ourselves. Some gestures certainly felt genuine in the beginning, but eventually fell short under the many guises of "justification".

Praying for us or sending encouragement cards seemed so genuine in the beginning. They helped, but by the end of our journey, these people had not visited Ed once. There were many excuses as to why, though they lived only a few suburbs away! For a long time, I found it hard to comprehend this until I realized it was fear: fear of death, fear of seeing a man in the prime of his life fading away, and fear of not knowing how to react.

It was hard for us to respond to someone who tried to give us hugs but never had anything to say. It was as if we had to understand how difficult it was for them. Awkward situations would invariably arise, creating an uncomfortable void in the form of a deafening silence. I, in particular, found it hard to deal with our ethnic community. When we were at a function, it was as if I could feel their eyes following us in silence across the room, their own fears dictating how they saw us, watching with pity, bewildered and wondering how we were coping. How staggeringly weighty this felt at times. There were occasions when it took all my courage to walk the length of a room full of these people. I wanted to run; I wanted to hide, to embrace my family, protect them, and whisk them away, from nothing more than feeling exposed, from being different and feeling vulnerable.

It was particularly hard to respond to someone who asked how we were and expected an emotionally charged reply. On many occasions we both felt at a loss for words in these circumstances. It was impossible to relate in a flash what we felt the day before, without it being in context. We were living in a constantly heightened state, like in a permanent crisis. How could we suddenly flick a switch to demonstrate a depth of feeling at someone's enquiry, for it had probably taken a mammoth effort to entrap it within our deeper selves in order simply to walk out into the world? It was as if we had to put on a performance and be perfect in all situations, our dignity and resilience were mechanisms to making everyone else feel "okay" about our situation. What was the correct response to someone who came up and said they could do my ironing or look after the children, especially when we barely knew the person who offered? Although, of course, I welcomed the concern, I needed to know the person somewhat. Surely, there had to be some initial dialogue to take the relationship to the next stage. When I look back I wish I could have perhaps responded differently. But both Ed and I were in a deep challenge. Ed's health issue was real, it was serious and unfortunately, it was with us every moment of every day.

My desire to continue to build bridges under seemingly impossible conditions was slowly failing, and I could see that other people felt the same. Instinctively I could feel that my energy was needed for my family and that is where I channelled my efforts. Unfortunately, Ed felt the brunt of my disillusionment, from exasperation to frustrated tears. We both dealt with our disappointments in different ways. Ed's reaction was passive: withdrawing into himself and allowing people to be as they chose, although in the end, he realised this had been a mistake and took a more definite stand. My response, on the other hand, was to withdraw into my family, to be proactive and concentrate on my children's needs and our journey.

Now suddenly, I was into self-protection, closing doors except to a few people. It was my coping mechanism, the only way I could protect my vulnerability and observe others flounder in theirs. Yes, my disappointments was obvious, I have always been good at showing that! It did not mean that I stopped all communication with people! No, it just meant that I became reserved and very cautious of what I said and how I said it.

This was not a pleasant place to be, and certainly my non verbal messages made things awkward for the people around us.

Our expectations were shattered three months into our life change, and I dealt with them the best way I knew how. It wasn't all despair. Along the way came people who reached out their hands to gather mine. To them I am grateful, for again I could open up in a way I had never dared to before (that was exciting) and be the person I really was and grow the way I had yearned.

With these people, I could relate my gripes; I could share my shortcomings strivings. They may not have understood I didn't expect that, for how could they? But they were patient and accepted my need to tell them and they respected my way of dealing with our situation, no matter how foreign it may have seemed to them. I was heading into new unchartered territory, a lonely journey of discovery.

CHAPTER 15

———— ❦ ————

LAST HOLIDAY

Fairy tale, fairy tale,
Where did you fly?
Away with the fairy dust
To yonder blue sky.
No more dreaming
No more scheming
Swirling mist gets in my eye.

It didn't take long for Ed's hands to lose their fine motor ability. A few month's after the diagnosis Ed's hand dexterity had deteriorated to the point that he could do up only the two middle buttons on his shirts. The top and the lower, as well as the sleeve buttons, became impossible. I kept encouraging Ed to try to persist with the buttons he could do up, but he soon found that even these were too hard. Yes, he was disheartened, but I didn't want him to lose hope, so I kept telling him what he could still do.

Soon, shaving became a problem as well. Here, the children were enlisted to help. I felt that, where possible, on the level that they could cope physically and emotionally, they should be involved, as it might help them come to terms with what was happening to their beloved Papa. So, they shaved their father each morning, lovingly, without complaint, and were happy to help, seeing his hand weakness as only a transient issue. There was a dedication, a commitment, to their father that ran deep without any conditions.

How we coped those mornings, I don't know. We each had our tasks, and they were carried out as best we each could. But it was only training for a far more arduous schedule later on. We all managed to leave home at our respective times, tidy, ready for the day, and with the house in order!

On reflection, this was the phase where the children adapted to their father's limitations insidiously. It was their first encounter, in their eyes, of their father being unable to do some tasks. Their unconditional love for their father was so palpable that, for Sebi and Lita, helping him was a means of repaying what they had received so openly from him. At this stage, they carried no resentment, no misgivings, just a beautiful, naïve acceptance. But their life was relatively simple in those early months, having no conscious sense of foreboding of what lay ahead. Their concepts of death and dying were remote and abstract. However, life was transforming them subtly. It took another six months before Sebi and Lita started exhibiting signs that their lives had changed. No longer were they carefree, childishly carefree.

In a moment of spontaneity, we decided to take our annual holiday up north. Was this to be our last family holiday? We decided to make the most of this one, desperately trying to keep our life normal where we could. Now looking back, this holiday took our life out of the ordinary, daily humdrum, where every day would seem the same. We all need highlights that prompt us to remember different parts of our life. This served to achieve just that, particularly for the children. It was a holiday of boogie boarding, fishing, fossicking, walking along the beach, enjoying the evening lights and watching the lighthouse beam its light as we ate our ice creams after dinner. Ed's legs were still quite strong and he was able to show the children how to find pippies at the beach while the tide was going out. We created quite an intrigue on the beach with our "pippie twist." Ed's legs were not strong enough to venture into the surf, so I played with Sebi and Lita in the water encouraging them to explore their abilities.

They were such enthusiastic children, finding life exciting, yet assessing it with a maturity that belied their years. It was always a thrill to watch them and marvel at their joie de vivre. How could I forget the morning after arriving at our holiday destination when I was woken by Sebi and Lita at six AM, standing in the doorway of our bedroom, all dressed in their wet suits, towels in hand, boogie boards by the door, ready to go! Oh, life could be good! All I wanted to do was take them by their hands and run. Run like the wind, run without a care in the world, run and feel their naivety, run and feel their freedom!

Yet there, beside me, lay my husband-my reality, and on my bedside table my latest reading material, *A Return to Love* by Marianne Williamson. No! All that could wait! And wait it did. We jumped out of bed, threw on our bathers and raced down to the beach to have an early morning swim. It was thrilling, carefree fun. It became quite a ritual in those two weeks and it helped to relieve some of the intensity of our lives and our seriousness.

We went walking along the beach coastline, clambering over rocks, exploring the beach further afield. It was here that Ed's already weakened legs suddenly became obvious when he lost his footing and fell badly. The awkward position of his fall meant that all three of us had to help him up. He was shaken and in a flash across his face, I saw fear, apprehension, and acknowledgement of his own predicament. This fall sliced into our idyllic but fragile holiday and reset the reality in which we were living! None of this was shared; only Ed's grazed face and hip needed our attention. After a rest, we continued, somewhat subdued, homeward

For me, it was my last holiday as a family where for a short while the realities of my life could be pushed aside relatively easily. For two short weeks, I was able to kid myself and the world metaphorically, that we were living a fairy tale that continued "happily ever after."

Our new life heightened the desperate lives we were leading trying to live up to some fairy tale image. Why? Fear! Fear to look, fear to question, fear to assess, fear to seek, fear to change, and fear to move on. Fear, fear, fear! Our lives are governed by fear. Fear paralyses us, immobilises our existence, and so we make the most of where we find ourselves, but we are never fully content, never realise life's potential and its wonderful gifts.

Oh, yes. I could have quite easily slotted into this fear rut. For rut it would have been, but I knew that soon it would have become a trench and, eventually, a grave where we would have each died our own death. No, I didn't want that! I did want to seek and did want to learn. No matter how difficult this journey would become, I had to learn to fly, to travel on those silver wings.

CHAPTER 16

---- ⚜ ----

HIGH HOPES

Life flashing by,
A myriad of sights
Like stardust on a sigh
Of half-forgotten delights.

My resolve for Ed's healing became absolute, but I was not blind to the enormity of our challenge. Deep within me, I began to acknowledge an awakening of true strength, an intuitive control that had been dormant for so long. This strength would continue to manifest itself, to carry my children and me through a most demanding learning curve, filled with bewilderment, anger, and ecstasy.

After our holiday, life returned to the usual bustle, but as Ed's health continued to deteriorate there was an urgency to continue seeking, finding, and applying what we felt would be of use in his healing process. Despite his health, Ed continued to work, meditate, and pray, but frustratingly for me, he still insisted on keeping his feelings locked away.

Meanwhile an Adelaide colleague of mine, Mark, together with fellow practitioners, had put together a technique that we felt could be of value to Ed. While in Adelaide we were also recommended to see a number of other practitioners. We made appointments with all these people, and then rang our good friends in Adelaide to see if we could impose on their hospitality for a number of days. This was all arranged.

Our stay in Adelaide was positive in so many ways. First, Mark felt that he could help Ed, although to ensure the body energy changes that he was endeavouring to bring about, Mark warned us that Ed would need to make frequent trips to Adelaide. Second, the other people we saw were also able to give Ed some insights into himself, as well as into our relationship. Those insights were accurate and gave both of us confirmation of issues governing our lives and a premonition of things to come. We were now entering the realms of energy healing.

We made the commitment to make the trips and Ed enjoyed all these sessions, but for me, there was an underlying niggle that kept gnawing away at me. It took a while longer for me to realise its essence.

Nevertheless, the two most lasting memories of this first stay in Adelaide are our friends' generosity of spirit and care and my children's naïve trust. Audris and Irene both seemed innately to know what to ask us, how to react, and how to deal with our situation. Yet, here were two people who had never before been confronted with such a situation. It was a relief to be with them, to savour their honesty. We all felt relaxed and protected enough to be ourselves, to lower our guard. Our children had been told the reason for our trip to Adelaide and accepted it without question. Papa's hands needed fixing! Each time we returned to Audris and Irene's home after a consultation, the children would grab Ed's hands to see if any change had already taken place. All I could do was hug and hold them and reassure them of my love. Ed made many independent trips to Adelaide leading up to Christmas 1995. He enjoyed these trips. Even though their main purpose was his healing, he revelled in the social aspect enormously. I would receive telephone calls or cards, by now in very poor writing, telling me what he had been up to. I was pleased for Ed, but the responsibility of keeping our household running, caring for two young children, and running a practice wore me down. I would vacillate between anger and relief, resentment and acceptance. Christmas was fast approaching and I had Lita's birthday to think about. I was feeling the strain of managing so many different aspects of life under such harsh circumstances.

Lita's birthday celebration was important to me. Despite all that was going on, I could not possibly allow this celebration to go unmarked!! I yearned to exhibit a sense of normality in our lives for the sake of the children, but also to ground me in my children's worldly needs.

In amongst all this, very occasionally, Ed's mother would ring and before long, would be criticising me, or Ed, or both of us. That would be my breaking point. After the telephone call, I would stand there shaking and in tears, the fatigue and anger overwhelming me, wondering why it had to be this way. Never did she ask how Ed was doing, let alone how I was coping, yet her ailments would be paramount. Oh how I craved some gentleness and care, to be cradled and held like a child against the elements of the world. Nevertheless, all I could do was to offload onto Samantha. It helped, but no one could comprehend the icy, vitriolic tirade that could burst forth from Ed's mother's lips. It was downright degrading, like being painfully hammered into the ground, hands flailing, desperately trying to come up for air.

It wasn't long after Christmas 1995 that I cried, "Enough is enough." I no longer wanted to deal with Ed's parents and I no longer wanted to interact with them. I no longer had the strength, commitment, or loyalty to continue to pursue a relationship that only brought about an agony within my heart that was now filled with raw pain of mammoth proportions.

Ed found it hard, psychologically, to write about his diagnosis to his father, who was living overseas. Ed felt there was no hurry to relay the news, as for many reasons, Ed's family lacked the art of communication. On eventually receiving the sad letter from Ed, his father rang Ed immediately, distraught and not understanding the full impact of the situation. Ed tried to explain this to him, but long distance phone calls never lend themselves well to intricate explanations or already-fragile bonds. It was soon obvious that the golden boy no longer had the same shine, and correspondence between them did not flourish as it could have to embrace what was still possible.

My decision to minimize contact with Ed's parents meant I was out on my own. It was my decision, not supported by Ed, who remained neutral, though he assured me that he understood. For me, my decision was liberating, exhilarating. I felt freer than I had felt in years. No need, anymore, to swallow their jibes or looks. For the first time, I felt the shackles of criticism start to fall away.

Notwithstanding all this, Lita's birthday was celebrated as usual, with children everywhere and family and friends eating, drinking, and talking. Even though tears flowed throughout the day, I steeled myself to what I desired for my family.

Christmas parties, Christmas, and New Year were all celebrated with family and friends as usual. Nothing was allowed to get in the way of what I was determined would be happy memories for my children. Yes, there were some altercations along the way, but I would not allow these to mar what I felt was important for my family's well-being.

For my family, I gave my all. I did whatever it took to create what in the past had come naturally.

A new year came and, with it, hope. Ed's achievements in Adelaide with Mark looked positive; there seemed to be some signs of physical improvement. The New Year started on a ray of hope, It was all I needed to renew my energy and to inspire me to maximize to the limit any healing that might be possible.

CHAPTER 17

CAMEOS OF LIFE

Window, window can I see
What is shining through your pane?
Do I see my memories flee?
But wait, free me of my pain.

There was no time to witness the excruciating emotions I was feeling. My emotions were like a volcano which could erupt spontaneously and abruptly without warning. Hot, sad feelings that were ever present. The pain would belch out from deep within me, powerful but transient. I did not allow myself to experience the full impact, which would have been my undoing. I longed for a mentor, an experienced hand to guide me through this minefield. In the meantime, there was no time for my personal issues, as there was so much to think about, to organize, and do.

Thankfully, the New Year of 1996 began with some lovely days at a beach house with friends and relatives. I have special memories of fun-filled days, relatively carefree. I took particular pleasure in watching Ed and the children enjoy each other's company, as well as their friends, trying to remember every detail of us all together. The children played cricket and Ed was the umpire, acting out the role of the famous Englishman, Dickie Bird. It was all very funny and there was lots of laughter. Oh, I hope the children can remember these times. There were so relatively few good times in their so short time with the man they idolized.

These days and others like them were a hiatus that gave me respite from the intensity of my chosen path. I was all things to everyone in my life, and that was the way I wanted it to be. At that time, I was not prepared to forfeit one aspect of my life to the betterment of another. All were important; all needed my energies.

Ed had arranged a father-and-son day of eel and freshwater Cray fishing with friends from Adelaide and Melbourne. It was a day filled with laughter, and they had many funny stories to recount at the end of the day. Ed liked holding court and being responsible for an event like this, and he did it very well.

We made the last trip to Adelaide in March. Mark explained he had helped Ed as much as he could; the rest was up to him. Ed and I both felt the culmination of the first nine months of our separate struggles with this illness. There was a real sense of what could be achieved if enough determination, passion, vision, and faith could be mustered. One only had to read about Dr Stephen Hawking's life, survivor of MND for over twenty years, to confirm what could be achieved.

But Ed was in some ways an enigma, who appeared to roll with the wave of life in an easy-going manner. He was not one to make splashes, just occasional ripples. He was affable and generally a pleaser, but he could also be stubborn. Like most of us, he found it hard to honour himself, to see himself worthy of making a stand. Many times, he pleased others, either family or friends, realising all too late that this did nothing for his own psychological well-being.

My dream was that this long weekend in Adelaide would be romantic and positive, holding great hope for the future. Unfortunately, it neither started that way nor finished on that note.

We had to partially change our arrangements, as my mother suddenly became unwell. I felt enormous pressure as I struggled to find a solution that would satisfy my mother's needs, my father's needs, as well as those of my husband. I did, and it all worked out well, though these situations always left me guilt stricken as if I hadn't quite resolved it fully, perfectly. Trying please everyone never works, but I went to great lengths to endeavour to do just that.

In Adelaide, I gave Audris a hard time for not finding a more romantic hotel for us, and I gave Ed a hard time for not being the romantic husband that I so longed for and dreamt about. The weekend consisted of a lovely lunch with our dear friends, visiting Mark several times, and watching on TV the election results that Ed was so interested in. Where were our dreams in all this? Lost, lost in the harshness of our life. All my frustrations, unfulfilled yearnings and longings came in on me, leaving me feeling as though life had nothing more to offer me and I could not expect more.

In the midst of all our life's vagaries, the harshness of life, the lost dreams, the never-realised dreams, came crashing in on me with regularity. These life incidents would pluck a raw nerve within me and have me crying for what I longed for, for what had never been satisfied.

I would frequently attempt to alleviate these tense moments by tickling either the children or Ed or, best of all, tickling and wrestling with my children on our bed. Mama would inevitably win and then there would be big disputes as to why, with great squeals about the time I was on the floor and that my tactics were totally unfair! That would go on until we were all laughing, exhausted, and it was time for bed and stories. These were cathartic times that helped release all our unspoken, half realized fears.

Oh, I enjoyed these times, as I know Ed did. As he became weaker, he felt less sure of his body. The psychological pressure of not being able to partake fully in these situations was overwhelming, and he preferred not to be a part of them.

I was constantly monitoring my children and Ed to see how they were faring. I would go to any lengths necessary to cajole them, to anger them, or to laugh them out of their bad moods.

This would lead to a sharing of feelings and, hopefully, to fewer unresolved emotions. This worked out well with the children, but Ed, as always and even more so now, was reluctant to show his feelings or even to realise what they were. He was more inclined to deal with everyday life rather than the deeper, darker underlying currents.

Prior to Easter 1996, I had an innate desire for a totally different Good Friday. The children and I attended our church regularly, and occasionally Ed would come along. He found it emotionally hard in church, and would often be reduced to tears. To him, it was embarrassing; exposing a side of himself that he didn't feel inclined to share.

On Good Friday, 1996, I told the children we would be attending a different church. They were curious as to where this church was and why they had to put on old clothes. Nevertheless, trusting their mother implicitly, they complied, and we left Ed at home, reading. We drove in the opposite direction from our church and were soon at a local beach. Still the children were confused. I raced them to the water's edge and chased them along the beach until they were totally confused and, suddenly, I began splashing them. They were only stunned for a moment, though! Next thing, we were splashing each other and became totally drenched.

It was good to feel the cold sea water on our bodies, it was good to feel the grit of the sand on our bare feet and hands, and it was good to feel the pale sun on our faces. It was raw and tingling. It was thrilling and made us feel alive! It was an affirmation of the life force around us that we needed to reconnect with in order to move on.

With Easter came the Sunday morning egg hunt. Soon after that, we travelled on our annual sojourn to the Grampians. The rugged mountain ranges of the Grampian National Park rise out of the flat rural plains over the Wimmera, marking the centre of this region situated west of Melbourne, not far from the South Australian border. The Grampians are renowned for their unspoilt beauty and stunning panoramic views, and we all looked forward to recharging ourselves.

The children, as always at the Grampians, lived in constant anticipation of each moment of every day with their friends. The Grampians were special to both Sebi and Lita, and to us. There were twenty children with whom to interact, friendships to forge and littler ones to nurture. By now, Ed's legs were weaker, though he did venture on a few of the easier walks. But the evenings were the times he really enjoyed and partook of fully. Sitting around the campfire, drinking, eating, and playing cards, he was in his element, laughing, making jokes, and enjoying the repartee amongst friends.

This life hiatus was soon over and reality again reared its ugly head. Nevertheless, I feel blessed to have these memories of Ed and of the children in our shared life that seems so short.

We had devised a paper clip arrangement for Ed's trouser fly in order for him to hook his thumb into this paper clip and therefore be able to manoeuvre the zip. Nevertheless, many times, I would receive a desperate phone call from Ed at work saying he couldn't do up his fly or couldn't pull up his trousers after going to the bathroom. He would break out into a cold sweat and this dilemma would completely unnerve him. He felt disinclined to ask his staff for help: pride, embarrassment. But there were times when he had to overcome these emotions and seek help, and it was always willingly given.

Ed would go to great lengths to explain to anyone what he was now incapable of doing, particularly around the house, although we all knew his limitations. We all wondered why he needed to do this. It was as if he had to affirm his own growing inadequacies and assimilate them into his psyche.

Ed's hand dexterity and strength continued to deteriorate slowly, and he suggested that we should make personal contact with the people at the Motor Neurone Disease Association's rooms to see what they could offer. Ed had already been in touch with the MND Association and was aware through Elizabeth, an MND

Carer Co-ordinator, what role the MND Association could play in our situation.

Elizabeth must have found me cold and reserved at this initial encounter. I found this visit confronting because of what might be ahead, and alien because it was not where I wanted to be. I didn't find the rooms welcoming, but rather depressing and unwelcoming. I'm sure a lack of money played a big role here. I now have no recollection of this time; I cannot recall either the location of the buildings nor what they looked like. I felt dismay and a sense of disorientation, just reinforcing my complete lack of wanting to accept our predicament.

I came out of these rooms angry, angry at myself, angry about what my family was going through, and angry at Ed for what he had. It wasn't the path I wanted to face and it and it wasn't what I had in mind. I was working so hard to turn this whole experience around. I felt I was the one doing all that was needed: making time for Ed to meditate, dressing him, taking care of his needs, boiling the Chinese herbs he was taking, giving him reading material, making suggestions, being positive, suggesting going to the park to play with the children, making sure he took his herbs, making sure the children spent time with their dad. Making, doing, suggesting, over and over. Doing, doing, doing, never stopping, I was like a wound-up clock, making sure everyone's needs were being met.

My life had become a kaleidoscope, not of colour but of responsibilities, each crying for my time, each carrying its own importance. It was my merry-go-round that, at times, I craved to jump off and run away from. These moments were short lived and, again, I would succumb to my daily tasks.

My fraternity's annual celebration was due and with it came the feeling that I could no longer attend. One of its mottoes was friendship. No doubt in the members' hearts, intent was very much there. A few even tried to show this, but my heart was broken observing the contrast between my life now and when my children were born. I had given so much of myself to this organisation and now I felt bereft. Times of adversity didn't seem to manifest this so-called friendship. I no longer felt amongst friends but, rather, bewildered and lost strangers.

Another hiatus: a few days of the school holidays were spent at the foothills of Mt Buller. The three of us did some horse riding, skiing, and bush walking. Ed had an upper respiratory tract infection at the time, always the fear of an MND sufferer, for their lung capacity diminishes due to muscle atrophy and their breathing becomes shallower. But Ed was feeling very positive and I could feel a new spark of hope in his attitude.

Soon after the school holidays, Sebi was meant to be attending an outdoor activities school camp, lasting three days. Sebi seemed to be looking forward to this new experience, but as the time for the camp drew nearer, we could sense that he was having second thoughts. He was anticipating his responsibility in the family. He felt that he might be needed while he was away. We tried to assure him otherwise, but to no avail. Five days prior to camp, Sebi came down with an upper respiratory tract infection and high fever. This infection was sufficient to ensure that he would be house bound.

I spent many hours discussing Sebi's situation with him, his teacher, our friends, my family and Ed, trying to resolve this problem. I felt distraught as to how to know the best solution to a terribly complex situation. I had sleepless, long nights. On the morning of departure, we decided to send Sebi with an assurance from us that, if his condition worsened, we would fetch him from the camp.

Sebi was an unhappy little boy leaving for camp, and a very angry boy on his return. It took him two hours of dialogue with me to release all the anger and frustration that he felt on being sent away. But by the time Ed arrived home from work, Sebi was able to put into perspective his time away and share with us some of the better times at the camp.

Ed was still driving, even though his illness was progressing relentlessly, and I am sure that, legally, he was well below his competence. A friend had devised a ball attachment to his steering wheel and, since it was an automatic transmission, Ed was able to manage quite well.

Sadly, it became harder for him to use his microscope at work due to his reduced finger dexterity, and all his notes had to be transcribed. His voice was also changing, but for his family, this was not initially apparent due to our every-day contact. He spoke more slowly, his voice did not carry as it used to, and a few sounds may have been harder to catch. His once loud amiable, rather high-pitched laugh became a gagged, uncontrolled laugh, as if some notes in his laugh were missing. Ed's legs were still relatively strong, but his gait was slower and slightly less steady. When he walked, his arms would hang, dangling by his sides. Notwithstanding his physical condition, his smile was still amiable, his demeanour assured.

Another lacuna-another holiday up north. We were snatching every morsel of life as we knew it. Unfortunately, due to our late arrangements, the only apartment available was a two storey one. It was far from ideal for us, as well as being half a kilometre from the beach. But there was a pool in the complex right outside our door, and this was perfect for the children.

Ed was no longer able to partake fully in certain physical activities. Using a knife and fork had become too difficult, though he could manage an implement in his right hand.

At our holiday apartment, I needed to help Ed up and down the stairs, with Ed leaning against the stair wall and sliding his shoulder, up or down, as the case may be, with me holding on to him. This felt precarious, and I was petrified that he would fall. Ed could not appreciate my extreme anxiety and became frustrated with me. He also found it baffling that I found it distressing to help him into the bath to shower him. He was a big man and his weight greatly exceeded mine. I would brace myself with each difficult situation, praying that nothing untoward would happen that would bring us both crashing to the floor.

On one of the many beautiful mornings at the beach, Ed being tempted by the stillness of the sea, decided he would like to go in for a dip. I felt unsure of this proposition but, wanting to please him, I complied. I only realised the strength of the water and its eddies when I had to help an unstable Ed into the water. He wanted to go in far enough that he could kneel so that the water level came past his chest. This I did but unsuccessfully as the pull of the water destabilised Ed and, momentarily, he became submerged. It took all my effort and what little he could muster to right him. Images raced through my mind of not being able to rescue him and get him out of the water. At these times and they were many and varied, I became angry for being put through such a stressful situation unnecessarily. In future, Ed sat in the shallows.

As always, our holiday passed quickly, with many highlights, including playing with the children at the beach or the pool, or cajoling Ed to interact with his children. There was shopping for provisions, meals to organize, and bedtime stories to read.

At the end of the two weeks, I felt empty, frustrated, and taken for granted. There was never any mention of appreciation for the effort that had been needed to bring this "holiday" about. Just a word would have made all the difference. It wasn't to be.

Shortly after our holiday, Ed's working life came to an end. For him, it was a multifaceted relief. The effort to prepare for work was becoming physically tedious, as was work itself. Not so much the microscopy, but the reporting, both written and verbal. Ed also no longer found himself morally compromised. His Catholic upbringing always had a bearing on his attitude towards terminations. If his results indicated an abnormality. this could lead to the prospective parents terminating the pregnancy. Ed was averse to this.

All of Ed's medical colleagues were shocked when they eventually found out the reason behind Ed's changed speech, but at last it all made sense to them. They had no need to surmise anymore.

There were farewells, there were promises to keep in touch, and there was a party in the park opposite Ed's workplace where he had enjoyed walking.

DR GUNTA KRUMINS-CALDWELL

Then it was all over, but with a promise of a new beginning. With another family, we celebrated with French champagne. We saw the life change as positive. Ed had purchased a new computer to use for emailing friends around the world. He also said that he would use the computer to write a book and letters to his children about his life experiences.

There was so much he could do, so much he could give. Sadly, surreptitiously, it became apparent to me that none of this would eventuate. Ed was playing with life as he often did, but he was not a participant.

Another Christmas was upon us, this time at our place. All the excitement, preparation, and anticipation could still be mustered. Father Christmas came with presents, there were presents under the tree, and there were cousins, family, and friends.

There was so much to live for, to cherish, to look forward to. It seemed to be fading, gradually fading away. Please don't fade! I want to hold on to every morsel of life that comes my way, to cherish and embrace it in my heart forever.

CHAPTER 18

MY TEACHER

In the dark corridors of my mind,
I see shadows lurking,
around corners flirting.
So easy to be blind
To all that I can find
In the corridors of my mind.

My first appointment with Erik is a blur. My emotional state would have been quite fragile, yet my mind eager and curious. My reserved nature in new situations concealed my defensiveness. What could this man offer? What could Ed and I hope to achieve with this man?

It was suggested that we visit Erik, for he had gifts and abilities that were beyond those of other psychotherapists. This certainly intrigued me, though, in the beginning, what really interested me was Erik's deep commitment and belief in God. Erik has a depth of wisdom and knowledge that is inspiring, coupled with the conviction that the mind, body, and soul are intricately balanced.

Erik, a tall Dane, is a man of true integrity who is, at times humbling and at others profound. He could be imposing yet shy, exuding a gentle authority. At times, he would just tilt his head with a quizzical look. He taught me the aspects of silence, be it for peace, awkwardness, discovery, understanding or wellbeing.

It was my hope that Erik could help us to uncover the reason or reasons why we were facing this crisis and, just as importantly, why we had "created" this condition.

The reading and work I had done even prior to 1995 had shown me that we truly are our own worst enemies, that we are the products of our emotions and how we address them.

Slowly, painfully but surely, Erik was able to take me through the corridors of my mind, to take me to half-realised truths, to take me to new ground, and help me through my spiritual wilderness. I resonated with this type of work. It was one-on-one and it was confronting but it felt liberating to delve into my innermost psyche and find out what was there. This was no easy task for me! It was frightening, it was awe inspiring, and it was humbling.

My meditations with the lessons in A Course of Miracles, which I had started some nine months prior to seeing Erik, were a substantial stepping stone. I had already developed a solid base in this area and my meditations could be quite exhilarating This, together with my reading up to date, gave me a broad perspective from which I wanted to journey further.

My urge to discover why I found myself in this predicament had propelled me to this point in my life by sheer persistence and the fear of being a failure.

Many times, Ed and I discussed with Erik, as well as with Aldis, our sense of failure. We felt like failures that we were in the situation we were in, and we felt like failures for not unearthing the reasons why.

Someone once described me as dogged. Yes, I suppose I had become dogged. Having found myself in one of life's larger crises, I was not about to wilt under the enormous pressure without doing my best to discover more about the deeper meanings of life. The outside pressures were many and could be summed up by the collective view, "What is the use?"

My dogged persistence exposed my inner strength. My inner strength revealed some ugly truths about my life, past and present, that I had pushed aside, not wanting to confront them. I discovered that we all want to so see our environment as supportive and nurturing. It is so sad when we discover otherwise.

We play games with ourselves and we play games with each other, just so we can live the illusion of life, governed by fear. It takes courage to face our demons and acknowledge them. It then takes more courage to face the next wave of battles in order to understand and learn what our demons have gifted us.

And battle I did. I battled both on a worldly level as well as on a spiritual level. To Aldis, I would say, for the sake of our children, I wanted to at least be seen to have done everything, everything that I possibly could to deal with this difficult journey. I was not concerned how much effort it took, nor how much money. I became dedicated to a deeper understanding of Life for me and my family.

My half-realised revelations about myself and about Ed helped me to understand more my life clearly and in greater depth, which in turn enabled me to help my children.

My spiritual awakening was even darker. Never did I believe that God in his wisdom had bestowed this crisis upon us. I could not blame God and take no responsibility. The responsibility was entirely mine. Could God, Who was infinite love, be so cruel? No, never! We attract what we have created; we give birth to what is manifest in our minds. I plummeted into a deep black hole, a black wilderness where I was on my own. I had to let go of God as my crutch; I had to grow up and liberate myself. I could confer with God, I needed to surrender to God, but I could not expect God to carry out my wishes. God was there as my counsel, as my comforter, but not to do my spiritual work for me.

Erik led me into this wilderness that I endured for many weeks, taking me through an array of illusions that were shattered along the way. Aldis was there to help me fill my emptiness with God's love. Erik was there to enlighten and guide me.

It was the blackest, hardest time in my life. I do not wish out of choice, to visit this period of my life again. The depth of despair was so great, so tangible.

The journey has been excruciatingly hard at times, but worth every tear that I have shed. My breadth of knowledge about myself and my fellow man and, therefore, of God was multiplied many folds. Though the pain lingers, it is a reminder of where I have been and why I find myself where I do.

CHAPTER 19

--- ❧ ---

REALISATION

Where is this world
That I so yearn
Of climbing trees
And scraping knees?
Why is my world
About to turn,
Disintegrate and burn?

The children's raw realisation of what was happening to their father suddenly hit them like a horrendous slap across their faces, which left them bereft, bewildered, and stunned.

They had been travelling so well, feeling reasonably positive, dealing with their father's situation remarkably philosophically. Yes, their father had developed physical handicaps, but he was still essentially their father. They were no longer involved with Ed's care, only occasionally helping when necessary. Nor could I take away their freedom and child needs in these circumstances. I was able to joke with them, help them with their homework, watch them, guide them.

A few days in early January 1997 were spent in Adelaide at a Latvian family seminar. During this time, the children were engrossed in organized activities with their friends and, in essence, spent only fleeting moments in the presence of their father. The following week, they spent at a children's camp without us. This was a new experience for them.

When we drove to pick up the children from camp, a few weeks had gone by where they had not had daily contact with their father.

It was so good seeing the children again, fun listening to their individual stories, both vying to be heard. The hour's journey home in the car went quickly as we took pleasure in our children's banter.

On arriving home, after sorting out camp clothes and putting the washing machine to work, we were anticipating spending the evening together watching a video and sharing a favourite takeaway meal.

A video evening and a takeaway meal or a favourite home-cooked meal was a way that we, as a family with restricted options, could spend time in each other's company. It had become a ritual that we all enjoyed and looked forward to.

With much discussion in the video shop, we eventually selected a video, White Fang, and then picked up our takeaway meal.

Most of life's profound realisations come about via a catalyst. For the children, it was this video: White Fang. The movie had just begun, our meal only partly eaten, when the mother wolf was killed, leaving the cub to survive on its own. What a metaphor!

This was Lita's emotional undoing, followed closely by Sebi's. Lita was in tears, saying she couldn't watch the movie; it was too heartbreaking, and she ran out of the room, sobbing. I followed and tried to console her. We both returned to discuss it with Ed and Sebi, but Lita was adamant that it was too ghastly. Ed became frustrated and angry, saying it was only a story, but this escalated the situation. Lita felt there was no sympathy for her, no tolerance for her reaction. Lita saw her father as not understanding her predicament and Sebi watched his father's baffling behaviour in bewilderment.

Somehow, I pacified everyone, although I was angry at Ed for his lack of perception of what was happening to his children.

We were able to finish our meal and finish watching the video, and, I thought we would be able to have a relatively early night to bed.

This was not to be! What followed was the start of what would go on for the next eighteen months.

Both children wanted to talk to me wanted to be hugged and held. They asked questions that we had purposely avoided up till then. Was their papa going to die? I was prepared for this question, at least. The timing was right; the reality had to be faced. We sat on the lounge room couch, hugging each other, coming to terms with what we already knew, but had not yet spoken about openly. Even though our covert time was over and there should have been a sense of relief, the air seemed to become even heavier, the weight of our journey even harder. It was as if our combined acknowledgement multiplied our burden many times over, rather than lightening it.

Sebi and Lita, both being very observant, had made a new assessment of their father after a two-week virtual absence. They could see the deterioration and the contrast starkly. No significant changes could be observed from two weeks prior, but the time away from their father now allowed them to focus clearly on the extent of his overall deterioration.

Ed's disabilities were no longer viewed as minor, but rather as an ongoing process.

Even though I no longer felt positive about Ed's recovery, I still held great hope that Ed would find the will, the spark, to live and help bring about a miracle. This was not what the children needed to hear, nor could they fully understand.

What I did tell them was that we must all eventually die some sooner than others. We are not, though, the only ones who determine when that will be. That is in God's hands as well. Why their father had this illness, I could not say, but it certainly wasn't God's will. Why we all had to go through this situation, I was not about to tell them, nor could they take everything in at once. Their journey had to be slow, unfolding in the gentlest possible way.

Yes. I did believe in miracles and, yes, I did think a miracle could bring about Papa's recovery, but it was not directly in my hands. The children wanted to know what they could do to help. I suggested that we could all pray as a family at the dinner table — pray for Papa's healing. They felt enthusiastic about this, and involved. There followed many months of dinner-time prayers, mainly related to Ed's healing, but I endeavoured to intermittently include all our trials so that the children felt that their personal issues were also being addressed.

By the time we had worked through their concerns, including why their papa had become angry, and had forgiven each other, it was midnight.

The children's realisation was now conscious. They were much wiser and more fully aware of their reality. They didn't know or need to know all the facts. With time, all would unfold before their eyes, if the deterioration continued. There was no need to place more of a challenge in front of them than was already there.

Suddenly, life was no longer simple, carefree, and happy. They had a burden to carry, to watch unfold every day of their young lives. There was no escape, no denying, no more illusions, just occasional reprieves spent with grandparents and cousins.

CHAPTER 20

―――― 🦊 ――――

THREE WISE MEN

Wise men bear gifts
Of frankincense, myrrh, and gold
Ed's wise men brought gifts
Of laughter, care, and love
In this cold world. How bold!

Ed often spoke about Stuart, Pat, and Moss. They were familiar to us well before we met them. Ed often recounted some funny or serious event that had been shared by one of the group in the course of their evening meditation.

We eventually met these three men when Ed could no longer drive. Tuesday evening meditations became an event in our house. We looked forward to seeing these kindly men who shared their week with Ed.

They were three very different personalities, each with his own hopes and challenges. Pat had a very sharp sense of humour, which at times verged on the sacrilegious. Being a thinking priest, he saw the farcical side of religion. The other priest, Stuart, saw the absurdity of some aspects of religion, no less sharply, yet was more tolerant of his fellow man's blindness. Moss, the youngest of the three, was a chaplain with an air of cheekiness about him.

This did not detract from his depth of knowledge or his wealth of experience with terminally ill people.

The four men complemented each other; their intellects equally pitted. They would banter with one another as only true friends can who feel compatible in each other's company. In an instant, in the middle of a discussion, they could focus on the other's needs and empathise with where the other found himself. It was true acknowledgement and deference to the others that was unconditional.

Each Tuesday, they would come with their chosen music and text of the week. They gathered in our study, where Ed was set up, sharing and lighting a candle to highlight their prayer. There was a level of trust amongst these four men that was a blessing to watch. Ed grew, both spiritually and emotionally, in the company of these men. He felt nurtured, cared for, and loved. I have no doubt the Stuart, Pat, and Moss did as well. All were so much richer for the time together. There was no judgment, no criticism, just acceptance.

Sebi and Lita always looked forward to seeing these three men. They all displayed an ongoing interest in the children which was much appreciated. All the focus seemed to be placed on Ed and his situation that at times left the children wondering where they fitted in. Here were three men who took the time to ask them how their week had been, how their music practice was going, or sometimes after listening to them play, commenting on how much their music had improved. They asked Sebi and Lita meaningful questions that required thoughtful answers. It was refreshing and it was genuine. Both children felt a deep respect for these men who were their father's friends. All of us felt an indebtedness and mindfulness of how much these three men brought to our family. It gave the children hope that, apart from family, there were people who could take the time to share just a moment of their lives.

There were times when I hadn't managed to organise Ed completely for the evening, or I felt so down that I could barely greet them each with a kiss. Nevertheless, they would quietly go about doing what was necessary without my asking. Sometimes, so little was said but so much was given. They were encouraging in their comments, empathic, and their sincerity uplifting.

CHAPTER 21

--- ❧ ---

NEW TERRAIN

Look, there's the road, it's just ahead
Through the mist, can you see?
Yes, the road it is still there.
Please don't flee.
Your light can shed
Upon the road a way.
Just try and you will see.

Who was this man who was battling along this most difficult of roads?

When first I met Ed, he was all intellect and no feelings. His feelings had been quashed many years before, in his childhood. Most people find it daunting either to relate or to listen to another's feelings. Best not to venture into the minefield of harsh words or softly spoken attempts to seek out another's comfort. We feel guilty, responsible, or repulsed, as the case may be, about another's feelings. What do we do with these feelings when we ourselves have little understanding of our own being? We seem to think that it takes skill to venture into this territory of feelings, when in fact it takes as little as just being. Being, and acknowledging another's dilemma.

There was so much unresolved anger and fear in Ed's family. It is easier to submerge your own feelings and learn to glide around these dark situations we call emotions.

Ed was affable; rarely did he create an argument, although he could become very angry if goaded enough. He loved to discuss and pit his detached intellect against anyone for the enjoyment of the experience. He did not want to prove that he was right, but he seldom moved from his point of view. This was his stubborn, inflexible streak that, with time, emerged more and more.

Ed was helpful as a friend and marriage partner, always willing to assist where possible and to his capacity, though asking was necessary. He was not able to initiate, yet, paradoxically in various organisations that he belonged to he always held a leadership role. This was partly brought about by his love of being the centre of attention. He was good in leadership roles, able to see clearly all the objectives, carry them through, delegate, and praise others for their efforts. Ed was respected and highly regarded, professionally and socially. All this sat well on Ed's broad shoulders, without too much ado.

Nevertheless, nothing compared with the love and admiration he felt for his children. Not always knowing how to relate to them, he was invariably the doting father. Ed thrived in this role. He felt it was the most worthwhile aspect of his life. Ed was determined to rear his children differently from how he was brought up.

We read extensively and had long discussions on child rearing. This was the one area where we rarely disagreed, we were a unified front until Ed's illness. We wanted our children to be brought up in a positive environment where emotions could be expressed without fear.

Ed had diverse tastes in food, wine, and music. Company came easy to him as he was a good conversationalist. Add to his love of following sport, playing cards, and fishing, and keeping up with current affairs, and it was easy for him to strike up a conversation with most people from any walk of life.

Yet Ed liked to flow with the currents of life as they moved him along. This meant that after his diagnosis, it was hard for him to find his footing in this new terrain where his life needed to be questioned:

how to deal with life emotionally and then how to translate this into the practicalities of everyday life. This illness was asking him to explore, to delve, to review. But, to Ed, it was as if he had begun to walk across a river. Suddenly, he found himself slipping knee-deep into murky, swirling tides as the water level continued to rise, with no sense of where to get a foot hold, to find shallow waters and move to the other side of the river.

There were no directions for his new journey, no one to follow. This was virgin territory. But Ed definitely had the potential to forge these new frontiers.

Ed made few attempts at asserting himself, even fewer in maintaining his stance where it could have mattered. He had his beliefs and points of view, and people were well aware of these, but honouring himself was another matter.

Not long after his diagnosis, Ed had his left ear pierced and, from then on, wore a stud earring, to the delight of our children. Their father had become cool! Ed had wanted an earring from his university days, but never had the courage to carry out his desire. He felt, by having this done now, he was acknowledging a latent yearning. It caused a few ripples amongst our families and friends, but maybe people become indulgently tolerant towards anyone in adverse circumstances.

Ed's normally accepting attitude was many times to the detriment of himself.

Such a situation arose when Ed had an appointment with the professor in his hospital rooms, to be told the results of his MRI. As Ed was waiting in the professor's rooms, the hospital neurology resident swaggered in. Without introducing himself properly, yet expecting Ed to defer to him, he remarked callously that the MRI showed nothing, so the diagnosis was unchanged. Ed was taken aback at this man's arrogant and demeaning way of relaying the results, knowing full well from Ed's medical history that his initial diagnosis was still very new. Ed felt as if the resident neurologist must think him a moron, with no intellect or feelings. He confronted the resident with the acerbic question of whether he was afraid to relate to him more humanely because he couldn't "cure" him. This time, it was the neurologist who was taken aback by such a response. When the professor walked in, Ed told him what had happened, but there it ended. Ed was not prepared to risk his relationship with the professor by insisting on an apology. This was a missed opportunity for all three to learn.

Ed's journey with a myriad of healers now began. Each played their role, from herbal therapy to body energy balancing to sound therapy to psychotherapy. Many were beneficial, some significantly. With most of the body energy therapies that Ed dealt with, he experienced either a temporary increase in physical energy or a sense of well-being.

One of these sessions revealed that Ed would experience a mild, transient depression every Thursday. He did not share this with me until, on one occasion, he was being treated by one such energy therapist who asked him what he didn't like about Thursdays. Ed said he didn't know, but he did confirm his depressed state. It suddenly struck me that both of Ed's diagnoses were made on a Wednesday, so the impact of these would certainly be felt on the Thursday. Ed had carried these symptoms for over twelve months. After this was corrected, he no longer suffered this depression on Thursdays.

Ed continued to pursue the various therapies in a methodical order, all suggested by me. He made no attempt to explore any healing methods of his own until November 1997 when, in desperation, I feel, he started exploring the internet about motor neurone disease.

The computer was a blessing for Ed once he stopped work. He could spend hours writing letters and emailing. The rest of the day, he would read or meditate, and when the children arrived home from school, he would help them with their homework and listen to them playing their musical instruments.

This all worked well for about twelve months. On the days that I worked, I would leave a sandwich on a plate covered with plastic film and Ed was able to manoeuvre it to remove the wrap and sit down at the dining table to have his lunch.

Ed's physical limitations were now far more obvious; in his gait, ability to use his hands, and even in his speech. The muscle wastage in his upper body, in particular his arms, was now pronounced.

I would shower Ed every night, as this was easier from a time management perspective, with less pressure on me to finish in a given time. The two nights of the week when I worked late and arrived home tired after nine PM were the hardest. By the time I said goodnight to the children, had my dinner and tidied up in the kitchen, it would be well after ten PM. During most of 1997, I would still, with Ed's help, get him into our shower, wash, dry, and dress him in his pyjamas, and put him to bed. This could take up to an hour, depending on whether I shaved him as well, and if there were no mishaps. I would be ever- vigilant of any imbalance leading to Ed falling or, worse, both of us. He needed to be dried quickly due to his reduced body mass. There were times I felt so angry, so frustrated with how my life was. I desperately wanted to share how I felt, to express what was bursting to be heard. Ed seemed so passive, so bereft of sharing his feelings with me. This only made it worse. Then I would feel guilty, burst into tears, and wonder why I didn't just get on with what had to be done. It would be easy to blame it all on my tiredness, but in truth, from a spiritual perspective, I was resisting surrendering to my circumstances.

In the mornings, I would attend to Ed's bathroom needs, dress him, and feed him breakfast before taking the children to school, and be at work by 8:45 AM.

April 1997 was the last time Ed came with us to the Grampians. I still wonder how I managed. Staying in cabins meant confined space and showers, but I still went through with all the tasks as at home. At times, I felt like a robot, carrying out my tasks day in, day out, with each task gradually becoming harder. I don't think I would have attempted any of this except for our children. It gave them something to look forward to and a pleasurable distraction for a few days. Ed did what he could from a gentle walk to playing cards with someone holding his hand. Now all his activities were thwarted by a body that was deteriorating.

Notwithstanding all this, he had an amazing capacity to enjoy the moment, to behave as though all was well. I would gaze at the scene before me in wonderment, for I could not imagine being able to behave in such a manner. At times, I had sheer admiration towards Ed, at others bewilderment, for all it did was put the other at ease; but it was artificial and out of place. Here, it seems, was a man intent on avoiding emotional discomfort where possible, avoiding the reality of what was confronting Ed, as well as the person he was relating to at that moment. Such contrasts.

He wanted to be involved in his life, although this did not always include us. He could stay in our study all day playing on his computer with little regard for his family and their needs. Yet he had the opportunity to do all his correspondence via the computer throughout the week. He was always willing to take part in whatever was planned, but he found it difficult to be the instigator, unless it was directly to do with his interests. Ed organized working bees to create a more maintenance-free garden for us, and he organized social outings for himself. Yet there were times I yearned for him to make suggestions for the family or to organize an occasion for us as a couple.

Ed always portrayed a positive image, ready to enjoy a joke or to take part in whatever was offered. He so wanted to take part in life. He was still young; there was so much to experience and I could see how desperately he wanted to be part of it all.

CHAPTER 22

———— ❧ ————

SEBI

Innocent and wise,
The observer of Life,
What can you surmise
In this world full of strife?
Cautious, caring,
Sensitive and brave.
So much blaring
But to this you are not a slave.

Even though Ed and I were in no hurry to have children after we married, our long term hope was to one day have a family.

We talked about what type of parents we wanted to be and how we would like to bring up our children. It didn't occur to us that it would take five long years to conceive with a lot of heartache along the way, especially when our friends started having their children and we had to come to terms with our disappointment.

Eventually, when Sebi did arrive, it was like all our dreams came true. Parenthood was wonderful; it added a new dimension to our lives, new meaning, and, apart from the sleepless nights, we were ecstatic in our new role. It was challenging, yes, but we were willing parties.

People would ring me at the hospital after Sebi's birth to inquire after our well-being, ask what name we had chosen, and what our new baby was like. After telling people we had chosen the name Sebastian, most times there was a silence. They were surprised by such an unusual name. It was obviously not Latvian! Then I would relate that Sebi had big hands, big feet, and a big mouth just like his father, and the moment would melt into laughter.

It was such a precious time, so full of hopes and dreams. When an acquaintance without children remarked some time later that parenthood was like a long, dark tunnel with light only at the end of twenty-one years, I was amazed at such a negative outlook. We were looking forward to this time with all that it entailed. Our only wish was to complete our family with at least one more child. Ed hoped that our second child would be a girl.

This big, chubby baby of ours grew into a beautiful boy. He loved music. From the time he was born, he liked us to rock him to music and, later, he would stand in front of the stereo, listen to the music, and clap his hands to the beat. He would use a wooden spoon to imitate a guitar and play while Lita and I danced to his time. When Sebi started school, he asked to play the piano. Before going to the States, Sebi wanted to start learning keyboard, as there was a van that came to his school from which people gave group lessons. Sebi was insistent, and we complied with his need to express himself through music. After our return from the States, a piano and formal lessons were organized. Sebi thrived in this area of his life enormously.

Sebi is an observer of life, from the beginning learning the lessons of life that came his way. He was constantly inquiring, constantly wanting to know and to assimilate. As a dear neighbour remarked, "This boy has been here before." Sebi showed early leadership yearnings, and the ability to assess people their strengths and weaknesses.

Sebi had an innocence about him that was endearing, yet a sureness of what he expected of himself. Often he would feel responsible for Lita's well-being and, later, was always mindful of carrying Grandma's shopping. He was not actively taught courtesies;

they just came naturally. That is not to say he couldn't assert himself or express his needs and wants. He could do all these very well.

Sebi always revelled in Ed's company. It could be eel fishing or freshwater craying, or it could be learning to ride his bike. He always looked up to this big man for his approval and encouragement. Later, it was maybe doing a school project together, Sebi with his ideas, and Ed with his suggestions and guiding comments. Big man, little man, bound by their gender.

Sebi has always taken life seriously, demanding much of himself. When the full impact of his father's illness became a conscious realisation, he had already started to prepare himself for the role he thought he had to play. Sebi, at the age of eight, felt that he had to take on the mantle of man of the house with all its responsibilities. At no time did either of us indicate that we expected this of him; he just felt the position had to be filled by him.

Sebi put enormous pressure on himself with this, but I had to let it be. This was his way of feeling that he was contributing positively to our family's journey.

Sebi has always been a child who needs to know everything in minute detail and in a chronological order. When he started school, he needed to know the full layout of the school, where everything was situated, and how the school was run. Once he understood it all, it would be processed and placed in his mind according to his needs.

Now the real possibility that his father could die left him bereft of where to start. He was a jumble of thoughts, emotions, and facts. How to place all these in the right sequence, how to make sense of it all? At the forefront of all this was this unbelievably excruciating pain, a pain that, at first, he could not even acknowledge for fear of completely breaking down. The pain was so deep, so encompassing, that it was overwhelming. To the outside world, no one knew what this boy was going through.

Slowly but surely, by reflective listening, I was able to help tease apart some of these raw emotions. There was anger, but on whom could he vent this anger? Sebi couldn't get angry at his father;

there was too much love there, too much admiration for this big nurturer. Towards his mother? No, that also was not possible, for he had remarked many times how much I was doing. At his sister? No! She was just another innocent bystander like himself. That only left one option. Anger at God! How could God do such a thing? How could God allow this to happen to the man he so dearly loved and cherished. Were we really so bad that we needed to be punished so severely? But then, how could there be a God? This world was evil; this world sucked!

How could I argue against any of this? He was expressing all the raw sentiments of our society, the collective. That is how most people react and see a situation such as this. There was no point in trying to change his mind or to reason with him. I could only be there for him and nurse him through his pain, his anger, and his exasperations. I would spend literally hours helping him work through his feelings and thoughts. I would suggest belting a pillow, imagining it to be God or papa, just so he could gradually move on to the next layer of emotions. Sebi found this hard for he is not aggressive by nature.

I would relate my own feelings of wanting to punch holes in walls, knock down doors, or, worse, hit his dad, just to alleviate some of my own pain. We would sit there on Sebi's bed holding each other, crying and talking until we were both completely exhausted and it was well past midnight. I would then drag myself off to bed, praying to God to have mercy on my child, to make his journey easier, to take away his pain.

But no! The next night would be the same, and the night after that and the night after that! Rarely was there any reprieve, rarely an earlier night. This would go on for weeks, then the long nights of talking would abate for a while, to restart some weeks later with a new set of emotions and thoughts.

It was a long, dark, tiring road. Every emotion of which we humans are capable was expressed and dealt with.

There were a few rare times when Sebi had a talk with his dad, but they were intellectual conversations; tears were held back, emotions hidden. Later, Sebi's emotions were expressed differently towards his dad. So we battled on until we felt like pulp, having been punched and bruised into a state of submission.

In the end, there was no more anger left, or any raw emotion that hadn't been turned inside out. Only tears were left. Sad tears. Tears of lost dreams, tears of robbed times, tears of acceptance.

CHAPTER 23

───── ❧ ─────

LIFE EXCERPTS

Flashes of Life
Once begotten
Long past
Not forgotten
Materialize these moments
Relive the memories
Please, just for a while longer.

Ed's life and our lives were changing rapidly now. Ed's restricted physical abilities had to be considered quite differently now. Quietly, somewhere between going to the Grampians and our annual few days in the snow, Ed's limitations began to require more care.

Ed himself was well aware of this. For the days when we went to the snow, Ed was able to arrange for his sister and his niece to take him into his niece's home and care for him.

There were feelings of concern for Ed as this was the first time we had sought respite for ourselves away from Ed. It gave me a vague sense of relief, a feeling of partial freedom and a temporary lightening of responsibilities. I was determined to make the most of our respite and enjoy the gift.

We had fun as a threesome, enjoying each other's company, as well as making daily calls to Ed. We stayed in the same lodge friends and acquaintances of ours. Were our friends afraid of us, confronted by us? It was incredible to observe. It was an acquaintance who helped us up the stairs with our provisions and our luggage, not our friends. They sat around the table amongst high pitched squeals of laughter, half ignoring us. I felt so lost and bewildered, yet I was in the midst of friends! I wish I had the ability to express to them what I felt, but it was easier just to observe. Out to dinner one night, one of the husbands ruffled his wife's hair to her consternation. Oh, if only my husband could be here and could ruffle my hair. Such small incidences carry such heavy messages of people's inadequacies and assumptions.

We had always been an active family enjoying such activities as bike riding, kicking a football or catching the waves at the beach. So teaching our children how to ski was just another activity we felt would bring them physical enjoyment that would help them appreciate their physical abilities as well as the gifts of nature.

Back in Melbourne, after our skiing interlude, there were increasingly limited interactive family times. Apart from our Friday evening video nights, what does a family do together in such circumstances? We would play board games or cards, with Ed indicating verbally his move, or we would sometimes go to the movies. We must have been quite a sight! I would hold onto Ed on one side and one of the children would hold onto Ed on the other. We would walk slowly as he shuffled along, barely able to hold his head upright without help. How did we feel? I think we were so locked into our world for emotional safety that we moved as one, as if in our own capsule of determination and resilience.

As the next school holidays were looming and my parents were in need of a break as much as we were, we decided we would attempt a holiday together. My parents felt extremely emotionally confronted by our life and had been helping where they could. Ed's physical health had reached such a point that the children and I could not manage anymore on our own in holiday circumstances.

Up to this point, Ed had refused to use the assistance of a wheelchair. I had suggested it several times after we had struggled on an outing, but his indomitable attitude did not want to succumb to the inevitable. It was only my father's suggestion that gave force to what I needed to organize.

Suddenly there was extra to do in a short space of time. Find a place to stay somewhere quiet with no stairs and not too many people around. Also, I had to see if we could find someone who was nearby and willing to hire out their piano in their house on a daily basis so Sebi could practice! He had a piano exam after the school holidays that still needed some preparation. Lita also had an exam pending, but thankfully for her it was easy: her flute was transportable.

The real estate agent took my requests seriously and even admonished me for not organizing all this sooner, for then we could have rented a house with a piano! Nevertheless, how interesting what people's perception is of requirements. On arrival, I was relieved that my parents would be with us, as the house was on stilts and there were at least twenty steps to deal with! True, the house inside was on one level, and the piano for hire was just a kilometre down the road! I was determined we would make the best of the situation.

When the long-awaited wheelchair was finally delivered to our home, instead of seeing it as an item of foreboding, the children embraced it as a plaything. They would take turns to sit in it and be wheeled about, trying out all the bits and pieces. Even though the wheelchair was old and basic, it was new to them. I observed in wonder these souls that could take something and turn it into an object of fun. That is not to say that they did not see the gravity of the situation. Far from it! But they made the most of the circumstances they found themselves in. It was a marvel to watch.

On this holiday journey, there were many incidents, some sad and some filled with laughter. They started when we realised after the taxi had dropped us off at the airport that we had left the wheelchair footplates in the taxi station wagon! With limited time before our plane took off, I had to track down the taxi driver and, hopefully, have the footplates returned in time. Thank goodness for my mobile phone! In the end, it was the taxi driver who kept hearing something metallic jangling in his station wagon and, upon investigation, brought the footplates back to the airport, just in time! Years ago, I would have been extremely worried how this could be resolved, but my trust in the Universe had grown. Now, I allowed God to take charge and I believed that, with some effort on my part, it would somehow work out. As it did!

The house we had rented was comfortable, the shower accessible to shower Ed, and the bathroom manageable. Only the outside stairs provoked feelings of dread each time we had to manoeuvre them, but with my father's help, we managed.

There are memories of Ed instructing the children how to make pancakes, amongst a tussle of wills. The children had their own ideas of how they wanted these pancakes made, with Ed insisting on his way. This had been Ed's specialty on a Sunday morning for a number of years, before his illness no longer allowed him this pleasure. We had barbecued fish that my parents and the children had caught. Here, they were instructed by their granddad how to clean and cook them. I went boogie boarding with the children and played hopscotch on the beach. We even took the wheelchair to the beach as the sand was so firm, and wheeled Ed along the water's edge. My mother insisted on cooking most of the meals, which left me with time to shower and shave Ed.

By now, Ed's body was really starting to struggle with gross neck muscle atrophy. The physiotherapist at the hospital he attended had organised a neck brace to support his head that could be easily adjusted and removed with Velcro. Initially, Ed used it only when his neck became very tired or when he was being wheeled in his wheelchair or helped to walk. His head would bob up and down as he was helped to walk to the beach, as we made sure his feet wouldn't catch on some rock or sand, awell as checking that our own footing was stable.

There are sad memories, as well. Not too many nights after arriving, I had to call for my father's help in the middle of the night because Ed had fallen out of bed and hit his head. Luckily there was no injury to Ed, but it was a shock for us both that dramatically changed the semblance of a carefree mood for many days. Going out as a family for a meal, putting Ed in his wheelchair and finding the right spot to sit and position the wheelchair required a sense that nothing could daunt us.

On our last morning, after breakfast, my parents had already left, and the children and I decided to go and say goodbye to the beach. We organized Ed in bed, saying we would be back within the hour. We had a lovely, frolicking time, jumping waves, collecting shells, splashing each other, and catching each other. As we were coming back, I sensed something was wrong and as we entered the house, it was confirmed. Ed was lying in a pool of urine with no way of helping himself except to partly roll on his side. How sharply it brought me back to our reality; how quickly our episode of fun was forgotten. How did I feel? There was duty, helplessness, empathy, guilt, and sadness all linked up together vibrating through every cell of my body.

Ed's hard journey was truly upon us. There was Lita's birthday, there was Christmas, all tinged with sadness, all weighed down by the heaviness we lived in. There I was, pulling this ever-heavier load, tending to all our needs as best I could by sheer willpower.

CHAPTER 24

———— ❧ ————

LITA

This flower, this bloom,
Must it open so soon?
It stands so pure,
Resiliently sure.
Fragile, it braves the element of Life.
It wants to dance
To be admired by chance
While living this life!

Lita came along in our life twenty short months after the birth of Sebi. She was wanted, she was impatiently awaited, and she came without a struggle.

This ball of chubbiness that had her first tantrum at ten weeks while I was changing her nappy! This baby bounced from the time her little legs had enough strength in my womb to catapult herself off my liver. When she was just five months old, she jumped and genuflected on my lap constantly. This baby needed to be strapped into her pram and was still able to do a Houdini and wriggle herself around. This beautiful baby would crawl out of the shop while Mama was trying something on. This innocent being could upturn a supermarket trolley as I was trying to rescue her body out of it.

This toddler did not like being number two sibling. She always felt as though she was missing out! This daughter warped all our drawers by swinging on them, and used my lipstick on herself and her clothes while I was at the other end of the house rescuing the clothes that had been sprayed with bleach!

This was a beautiful girl and I took pride in dressing her up before going to see friends, only to find her, five minutes after arrival, running around naked, free as a bird! She was this strong soul whom I would ask to do a simple task, but who would become distracted along the way and start to play. On being asked why she didn't do as she was told, she would look surprised and exclaim that she had the urge to play

How did I learn to contain this free spirit who was wise beyond her years, who could observe, assess, and then dismiss. She was not one to dwell on the negative, and not one to worry about the consequences. Consequences could wait until a chin needed steristripping or a finger needed rescuing after being jammed in a door. The drama could wait, but when it had to be lived; it was heard by all.

This little girl needed to chat and found a good ear in Grandma. This little girl also needed peace, away from the bustle of crowds. This little girl has a lithe, long body full of grace and with a sureness about her feminine spirit!

How Lita loved to be tickled by her papa, to sit on his knee, to put her head on his shoulder. Seeing the love in her eyes as papa chased her or threw her in the air delighted me. This big man and this little girl had a mutual admiration for each other for all to see.

How does a free spirit cope when her world is turned upside down, when what was real no longer exists, and what could not be imagined was unfolding before her eyes.

Lita was never one to ruminate or catalogue her thoughts in a logical way. She scans a situation, assesses it, forms a conclusion, and deals with it accordingly, all within a matter of minutes. No point in looking at it from every angle when, to her, it is plain how she sees it. Unfortunately, her father's illness left her floundering to identify how best to deal with a situation that was unfolding every day of her young life with the man she wanted to be with.

Lita's emotions would gradually build up until she could no longer deal with them herself. It could be about how her father would die or concern about why we were going through so much pain and no one else was there she could relate to with her emotional pain. There was no one that we knew who was going through anything remotely like what we were. Yet, she naturally had expectations of how she would like others to behave towards her.

How does a mother console her child with such an array of adult conflicts and emotions? At intervals, she would give it all to me. Lita would express her fears, her disappointments, and her confusion about what was unfolding before her eyes, then hope I could help her through her thought processes, quickly and to the point. This I would do to the best of my ability, but there were times when it took a while. Either I couldn't find the right words that made sense to her, or my way of looking at the situation was not hers. I would flounder and feel inadequate trying to reach this little soul whose being was in so much pain. There was agony in my heart, watching Lita being swallowed up in her pain, for this created bewilderment and ineptness in me.

Lita's pain gradually built up like a golden rod deep within her. This became her reality. If Lita could hang on to this, she could survive. Lita's searing emotions engulfed her at times as she battled with relationship issues at school, finding little comfort in friendships. Lita hurt herself frequently to keep in touch with the physicality of pain.

Pain was Lita's companion. At times, it was frightening to watch her seek comfort within this realm, but I had to allow her the freedom to find her own way of dealing with her journey. Ever vigilant of where Lita found herself, I was always ready to comfort her. But many times, there was no comforting her, Lita would find human contact too confronting. This little soul was painfully watching her papa, her idol, slowly withering away.

CHAPTER 25

―――――― ❧ ――――――

CARERS AND ROSTERS

A stream of people at our door,
It's not locked, so come on through.
Carers, physios, OTs and more
Pastoral, GP, social worker what's more,
As well as MND volunteers to see us through
All with a purpose, all here to assist
My home-open house to them all.

Surreptitiously, our life changed. Life was no longer our own; home was not our private domain. We became exposed for everyone to see. Into our life appeared Terry, our case manager. Without her and the Motor Neurone Disease Association, our life would have become completely untenable.

Ed had organised meetings at regular intervals with the MND Association to ensure that the appropriate help would be available when it became necessary.

At the beginning of this time, a carer would come in a few times a week to take the pressure off me on the days that I worked. It was a welcome relief, as the intensity of our situation due to Ed's continuing deterioration had an overwhelming effect on our family, even from a purely practical aspect. I was becoming emotionally and physically drained, at times wondering how I could cope. As a result, my behaviour could be abrupt and tactless.

The carers who were familiar with MND sufferers could be left to attend to Ed's needs with only a few suggestions. Unfortunately, the agency carers sometimes were completely unversed with Ed's incapacities, having only dealt with the elderly or with people with minor disabilities.

I found it frustrating, incomprehensible, and tiring to have to teach these carers about MND and its consequences on the body and how to best manage a body that was virtually incapable of helping itself. I would go through all the aspects of Ed's needs and wonder if it would be easier and quicker to do it myself. Then I would pull myself up and presume that when this carer knew what to do, the load for me would be easier. But many times, no sooner was the carer adept at their job then it would all become too hard for them and they would leave.

It appears our society has such a long journey of learning to reach the point where we can embrace with empathy those less fortunate. Sympathy seems to be the most we can muster at our best. At our worst, we seem to be embarrassingly inept in our dialogue, body language, and in our actions.

Very little thought is given to what effect a wrong comment can have on someone in Ed's position. One carer, wheeling Ed into the bathroom, commented on Ed's lack of cheerfulness, herself obviously feeling in good spirits. Ed, no longer able to come back with a quick rebuttal due to limited facial muscles, left me to comment, as I was drying my hair, that maybe due to his circumstances he felt there was nothing to be cheerful about at that moment. It was an innocent comment, probably well meant, but it was so out of place.

Certainly, there were carers with an innate sense of a person's circumstances who performed their role admirably, with a lot of thought and care going into their time with Ed.

What at the start of November 1997 took a carer one hour to tend to all of Ed's needs in the morning, by September 1998 took two and a half hours. The tasks would seem simple. Get Ed out of bed, toiled, shaved, teeth brushed, showered, dressed, fed breakfast, and then organised, either at the computer or in his recliner.

But each task took either a great deal of effort and manoeuvring, or had to be done slowly and gently. Great patience was required on the part of the carer, particularly in the last six months when Ed could no longer communicate verbally. A baby would have been easier to manage than Ed.

I remember spending over two hours with a carer who was not versed in any disability attendant care, just going through Ed's detailed requirements. My patience was tried as I could not comprehend how a carer had no remote sense of what was necessary. This same scenario was also played out many times at the hospital and hospice Ed stayed at.

Is it possible that people switch off their feelings, do they act out their professional roles like robots, and do they go through the motions of their allotted tasks without thought?

Ed was a master of his emotions, with reasonable self esteem to deal with these situations, and if he wasn't, due to his incapacities, then I would step in. What happens to people less able to deal emotionally with these situations due to their poor self esteem? How do they cope in such circumstances? As well, most people are floundering just to come to terms with their terminal illness.

Do we live such fragile, insular existences that we cannot afford to imagine ourselves in similar circumstances and how we would like to be treated? Surely it is every person's inalienable right to be treated with all the care, love, and compassion that are required. Surely there should be no justification, no excuses. Care does not cost money, but it does confront one's own ability to deal with terminal illness and death.

Choosing to care professionally for another asks, in the calling, for a level of understanding, the ability to grasp not only what the patient may be going through but also their family's needs.

There were times when I had to confront the agency manager because I felt she was not training her staff of carers, and was not aware of their weaknesses, such as when a carer came late several times due to oversleeping, or didn't turn up at all. If on any occasion. I knew there would not be a carer, I could adjust my day accordingly and adapt. But when someone does not turn up at the right time, it becomes a mystery to know what to do. How many times I would wonder, do I start organising Ed myself or wait.

Many times I was in tears after numerous phone calls, trying to find out what had happened to a particular carer. It was a nightmare of impotence on my part. How could someone say they needed the night off at the last moment or they didn't feel like working, or lie by saying they had told the manager they would not be working on a particular night. These were the times I would break out! After several quite distraught verbal interactions with the agency manager, I would either find myself eating a whole packet of Tim Tam biscuits (they really do satisfy the emotional distress) or, on one occasion, sitting in my car staring blankly out the window and having four ice-cream Magnums, one after another. Yes, I would feel sickly afterwards, but strangely comforted.

Terry was there to pacify me, smooth out the dilemmas, and rectify the situation. She was invaluable! Terry's placatory manner invariably appeased my distraught sense of hopelessness. She would soothe me, pacify me, and acknowledge my dilemma, and just go about correcting the situation. She would follow through each time and recommend the necessary changes. It was Terry who was able to find the funding for a page turner. This page turner was a blessing for Ed who was an avid reader. There was a three-month period when Ed could no longer sit at computer unassisted and it was impossible for him to turn book pages. Throughout this period, he would just lie back in his recliner and watch taped films or videos.

Ed's first stay in hospital to give us respite was in January 1998. It was a sad learning curve for us both. On visiting Ed a day after he had been admitted, I walked past the nurse's station, where ten nurses chatted and laughed vigorously. At the time, it went through my mind that the ward must be half empty for so many staff to be able to spend time during working hours talking. I soon found out that this was not the case, that in actual fact, the ward was full!

I found Ed in his room sitting in his wheel chair turned towards the window. It must be one of my saddest memories of Ed. There was no radio, no TV, no one to converse with. He'd been just left. After enquiring why he was left like this, he said he did not know. He said he had tried to organise a TV, but no one had followed through. Ed also recounted that, after being admitted the previous day, he had been left in his wheelchair for four hours unattended; I was astounded and mortified. This was no respite for either Ed or me. How could anyone do this to someone in Ed's position? There were twenty-eight patients in this ward. Did that mean they were all being treated the same way! I went about organising a TV and spoke to the floor manager. All would be done, I was told. On leaving, I observed that the nurses' station was still crowded with them giggling and chatting to each other and appearing to be having a good time.

Some time after arriving home, I felt it would be wise to ring the hospital to be assured that all had been arranged. To my consternation, Ed had not been moved and a TV had not been organised. Again I felt impotent and outraged and, on speaking to the floor manager, all he could offer in mitigation was that he was new and it was hard changing nursing staffs' attitudes!

Conscience, integrity, care, empathy. So much was lacking, so much that required so little. We seem to be a society asleep to the needs and welfare of others. It is so easy to give money when collections come around. It takes nothing, no time, no effort. We are in dire need of becoming a community again, to seek out, to enquire, to be proactive to another's needs. Where has all this gone in our materialistic world?

After Ed's stay at the hospital, we were fortunate to have arranged for him a hospice that was more familiar with MND. This worked so much better, and improved as staff came to know this man, though Ed would recount a few horror stories, nonetheless.

By March 1998, Ed was using an alphabet board and a laser pointer on a cap that he wore, to spell out his requirements and to converse. Most of the time this was successful, but there were staff who would ignore this set-up and go about attending to Ed according to their own schedule and needs, with no regard to Ed. Ed liked to stay up late while at the hospice and watch the foreign language channel movies. This was his luxury, for at home a carer or I would put him to bed at a time that was convenient to both of us. In the hospice, it made no difference, for there was staff attending around the clock. Ed was not fussed if he was put to bed at eleven thirty PM or twelve thirty AM, if that fitted in with the staff routine, as long as there was something watch or read. So, he was not creating an inconvenience, just wanting some freedom. We both felt baffled by such a dogmatic approach when it was unnecessary. On arrival at the hospice, at the ambulance entrance, we would lumber in, with all of Ed's requirements. It would take me in excess of an hour to set Ed up in his room with everything he needed.

On one occasion, as I was trying to manage all this, a staff member waltzed in, bleary-eyed, commenting to another nurse that she had had a great night out, but very late. She wondered where the page turner was that she was supposed to help set up for this patient. There it was beside her! No, she didn't see it, and waltzed right out. These were silly incidents and, in the context of life, not that important; but hurtful, nonetheless. Again, there was bewilderment on both our parts. All I could do was shake my head and continue setting up. I couldn't say too much for fear of upsetting the staff in such a way that there would be negative ramifications for Ed. What a bind, such a power play!

A much more serious situation arose when Ed was in bed at the hospice and in need of the bathroom and his alarm was out of his reach. A nurse had looked in to Ed's room from the door, asked if all was well and, getting no reply, continued on completely unaware of the seriousness of Ed's condition and trouble he had communicating! Ed was exasperated and, with no alphabet board set up, could only close and open his eyes to a question. How desperate he must have felt, how impotent, how full of anguish, locked in a useless body with all his faculties as sharp as ever. Still so keen to be a part of life, still so curious.

CHAPTER 26

AN ORDINARY WEEK

Planning, organising, rushing, doing,
What's that I missed.
Should I assist?
Talking, resolving, worrying, smoothing,
I hope it's for the best.
So tired, so tired
But no time to stop
Everyone needs me.
When will it stop.

Monday

My long working day was an easier day to cope with than being at home with Ed. It may seem strange to view it this way, but I become immersed in my patients' problems. Working tends to put my own problems into perspective. This seems simpler than constantly tackling my own.

I always try to start my day at six AM with a meditation. This is my time with God, my time to resolve my latest challenge, my time to have some insight into my journey. In the mornings, it can be an hour. In the evenings, it is much shorter, as I am so tired.

Monday mornings are easier, as a carer comes in to tend Ed's needs and feed him. This carer is reliable; I know she will to turn up. She arrives before we leave. Ed's breakfast is on the table, and the newspaper was put out so he can read while being fed. Lunch is in the fridge with instructions on the bench top for whoever is coming in to feed Ed today.

Lita seems positive about school this morning. I sometimes wonder how she does it. But she is philosophical and is able to process life's lessons very well. She's amazing.

Busy day at work, but good. My patients are now aware of my home situation. Very tactfully and caringly, each in their own way, they make regular enquiries as to how I am coping and how things are going. They make complimentary remarks about how amazed they are that I can still work, that I am not distracted, that I always look so well and am immaculately groomed. I accept the compliments. But there are times when friends remark with the innuendo that I look too good and too well in my circumstances. They look suspicious. How could I possibly look this way in my situation? I know it is their projection, but it is hurtful, nonetheless. My only response to these comments is a shrug of the shoulders and a reply that God is guiding me. don't think it makes sense to them. At other times, when I am not feeling so positive, I feel like crying out and saying, please just give me an unconditional hug. Don't judge me or condemn me for the way I am dealing with my situation. God knows I am doing the very best that I know how.

The day goes by quickly and soon it is three PM, time to pick up Lita. Sebi is at camp, so that's one less trip. We arrive home just as my parents are pulling up in their car. The children are always pleased to see them. My parents have been coming for some time now to take the pressure off our nanny and Ed. Ed is no longer able to exhibit a sense of authority with the children. Sebi and Lita are finding Ed's deteriorating condition increasingly stressful and they are starting to become unruly. Our nanny is not able to deal with all this, either. This was another situation that was brought to my attention slowly, as I gradually realised things were not working out and that wild chaos was developing.

My parents' presence brings stability into the household while I'm not there. The meals are rather modified to what Ed can eat, though there are variations that satisfy both Ed and rest of the family. The meals are always pre-prepared by me, with just the need for a salad or vegetables to complete them. I don't want to overexert my mother, as I am just grateful they can be there until I get home.

I go into the study to see how Ed is doing, only to find that the condom urinary bag that he now wears was not closed off at the end by the carer; his shoe is full of urine and the floor is flooded. It is now 4:05 PM, and I should be at work again by four thirty. I don't deal with these situations very well and they seem to come up rather frequently.

My never-ending lessons. I get angry and frustrated at the apparent lack of competence on the part of the carer. I get angry at myself, I get angry at Ed, and I feel at the end of my tether. I feel out of control, yet needing to be completely in control. I don't want to be! I want to run away, run away, run away!

Now I have to wheel Ed in his chair to the bathroom, manoeuvre him off the chair onto the toilet over which I have placed the raised seat, as he has also indicated that he needs to move his bowels. So while he is sitting on the toilet, I take off his shoes, socks, and trousers, as they have also become wet in the process. I am trying to work at lightning speed. Readjust the urinary bag, strap it on, clean socks, undies, sandals, and track pants. Clean Ed, pull him up to an upright posture, and then dress him. I then slowly help him to his chair. Once he is seated, I call out to my father and Sebi to take over. It is 4:25 PM and I have to rush off to work. I won't make it in time, but I'll ring on the way and let the receptionist know I'm running late. Hopefully, it will work out.

Tuesday

The alarm goes off at 6:10 AM. Is it morning already? I feel so tired, I can hardly keep my eyes open. Hectic day at work yesterday, some receptionist problems, as well as the usual home situation. Being too tired to talk to God, I read and contemplate on my inspirational text. A poor second best for me, but at least I will have flashes during the day of what I have read. Always relevant.

I have only Lita to get to school today; this helps slightly. After my own morning necessities, I get Ed out of bed, attend to his bathroom needs, dress him, feed him, give him breakfast, and then organise him in front of his computer.

By eight AM, we are out of the house and on our way. I talk to Lita about school friendships and her bad moods. She had another one this morning. Lita eventually explains that Ed had a choking fit last night for half an hour at the dinner table. He was not able to eat and apparently became "grumpy." My poor Litty! It's so hard, so very hard. She desperately wants to be with her papa but, at the same time, is vying to run away from the enormity of the situation. Luckily my parents were there. At least they try very hard to diffuse the heavy atmosphere and my father is good at telling jokes that the children enjoy. But I find out that my mother is not eating while feeding Ed nor afterwards, so is going home without a meal. I will have to arrange for a carer to come in and feed Ed, as this is putting too much psychological pressure on my mother. If only I had known earlier! It didn't even cross my mind that this was a problem.

We arrive at Lita's school by eight thirty AM. I let her out and, as I have half an hour to spare before Lita's flute lesson, I whiz up to the nearby shops to buy my parents flowers, as it is their wedding anniversary. With still a few minutes to spare, I have a quick coffee.

Now, back to school for Lita's flute lesson.

On my way home, I call Aldis, as he had left a message on our answering machine to contact him. I arrange with him to come by our place on the following Monday to see Ed. I must remember to tell Ed. I have reached a point where there is no time to reflect on the myriad of daily challenges. I do what needs to be done when it arises, and each new situation feels like another mountain that needs to be scaled. I feel battle-weary.

I get home to sign cheques that Ed's former secretary is writing out for outstanding bills. (Joan came in once a month voluntarily to help us out with our paperwork). While Joan is doing this, I check the answering machine to find that Sebi's school psychologist has rung and asked if I could ring her. I try to ring her, but get her voicemail, so I leave a message. Hopefully, she will ring back soon.

In the meantime, I put away a basket of ironing that has been brought back by the ironing lady, answer Joan's queries, and answer the ringing phone. This time, it is Sebi's school psychologist. She tells me what she spoke to Sebi about and that, on a few occasions, tears rose in his eyes as he was telling her the sadness he feels about his father's illness. Also, she said that he said he is able to talk to me about it. She praises us about Sebi, telling me he is a beautiful boy, well-balanced and, considering his circumstances, doing remarkably well. This brings tears to my eyes. My constantly aching heart lets out a cry of agony at the thought of my boy sitting with a stranger, trying to put words to his deeply painful feelings. Then the front door bell rings.

The gardener has arrived to talk about how often I want him to come to mow the lawns. Joan handles him while I pull myself together. I feel like a jack-in-the-box, feelings pulled out, feelings sucked in. I can't do it, but I must! Next, I talk to the gardener about when he would be able to come on a regular basis.

It is now after eleven AM. Time is running on and there is another phone call. This time it is Anita ringing to see if by some chance we could get Ed to court on Thursday when her husband will be sworn in as a judge. Anita suggests what seems like a complicated arrangement, which I then need to run past Ed, who in the meantime has tried to arrange through Joan for a friend to take him. So now I have to wait and see how this will pan out. Oh help. Which way do I turn?

I then load Ed's wheelchair into the station wagon, with all its bits and pieces: headrest cushion, foot plates. I toilet Ed and, eventually, slowly get him into the car. It is now 11:50 AM and we are running late.

I drive to my parents place, some twenty minutes away, to deliver the flowers and champagne, and then to the hospital where Ed has three back-to-back appointments: a physio and two separate neurologists.

Ed's attending neurologist, as always, is straight-faced with barely a smile, just checking to see how everything is going. I feel like demanding to know what she is feeling. Does she have any feelings and if she has, what are they? Perhaps she leaves them at home neatly folded in a cupboard until she gets home and puts them on with her track suit? Or, does she keep them in her office drawer to be aired only with colleagues. I do not believe conveying some feeling would diminish her professionalism; it would not make her a lesser practitioner. But the fear monster, it seems, keeps the door tightly closed. It's much safer that way.

On the way home, I get some keys cut and buy bread for tomorrow's sandwiches.

At home, I get Ed toileted and sitting in his chair with a new pump-up cushion that takes some adjusting to get right. Then I organise a video film for Ed to watch prior to leaving to pick up Lita. Before I leave, I take the washing off the line and fold it. This is all done on automatic pilot and as quickly as possible.

On collecting Lita, I am delighted to find out that she has had a good day at school for a change and she is happy with the girls. She agrees that the girls are like the wind, changeable. I suggest to her that maybe she could be the tree that is forever able to accommodate the direction of the wind. She nods in sad agreement. Oh please, don't be sad Lita. I long to see your carefree face again. I want to see your beautiful smile and a body that is restless with the joys of life. But no, these are all gone, having fled, only to be replaced by a burden on these small shoulders that is weighing her down.

At home, there are more phone calls, patients who need appointments arranged. I make tomorrow's sandwiches and organise dinner while helping Lita with her homework problem. We start dinner just after six PM. Ed's meditation group will be arriving at seven thirty PM, so time is limited.

After Lita finished her dinner, I send her off for a shower while I continue to feed Ed. I ring the necessary people to see if some arrangements can be made to get Ed to the court on Thursday. Eventually this all falls through, and Ed decides it is too hard for everyone and gives up the idea. Then a few more phone calls to rearrange who is feeding Ed on Thursday, but it doesn't work out.

This has all taken well over an hour and a half, so Pat, Stuart, and Moss arrive as Ed is still finishing his meal. Quietly, they go about setting up for the meditation, innately realising that my day has been anything but easy. Thank God they have the courage to respect me. I then get Ed organised for his meditation, seated and comfortable. Eventually the kitchen is cleaned up and Lita announces she wants to do a fashion parade for me. I sit and watch. Suddenly I remember I still have to arrange for a friend to feed Ed on Thursday, so I rush of to organise that! Lita continued her fashion parade. At eight thirty PM, it is time for her to go to bed. As always, I read to her a bedtime story and just about fall asleep myself.

Then at 9:10 PM, the meditation is over and it is time to get Ed organised for bed. By 10:30, all is done.

Another day! No different from the rest, just different tasks to do. I become so frustrated; it feels thankless. Where does all this frustration come from? It seems like a bottomless well that keeps spurting up the same, over and over again. Erik tells me to do it for God. At times it is so very hard, but I must keep going, must keep challenging myself to accept it all.

Wednesday

Today is only a half day of work. Then I have to take Ed to the dentist in the afternoon. He has insisted, though the tooth is not hurting and, on speaking to the dentist, I was told the tooth could be left.

Getting Ed from the front door to the car takes all my strength, patience, prayers, and judgment. A ramp is being organised, but that will still take some time. In the meantime, Ed has to prop his body against the front door frame while I'm holding him by the arms, then slowly drop one foot down the step to the veranda. With his back against the door frame, he pulls the other foot over the step to the veranda. I have already opened the car door, and now with one more step down, I have to twist Ed around, still holding him firmly by the arms and very slowly lower him into the car, making sure he doesn't hit his head or hurt his back. I then have to lift his legs into the car, strap him in, and place a cushion behind his neck with his neck brace on.

I must drive carefully with no heavy braking, as this throws Ed's head forward due to the deterioration of his neck muscles. I don't always achieve this and I can tell that this annoys Ed.

At the dentist, I want to drive the car into the drive to make it easier for me and less distance to the front entrance. Ed is not happy with this and wants the car left on the street. Unbelievably we have an argument about this, as in my view it is a lot harder from the street than the driveway. Ed also insists on where the car should be parked. I point out that there are branches on the nature strip and it won't be easy to get around them for him or for me. Can I at least drive slightly along where there are no obstacles? Ed is not happy with this either. I am totally exasperated, but comply. I struggle to get Ed out of the car and we shuffle to the front entrance. There are two steps. With each one, it takes a mammoth effort to get him up these small steps. Inside, it is not easy to get him seated, nor to hold his mouth open or control his tongue while the dentist is conducting her examination. The whole situation is fraught with extreme difficulty with no real achievement. The dentist is not prepared to drill, doesn't feel it appropriate, and puts in a temporary filling. Now I have to get Ed out of the chair and retrace our steps back to the car. By now I am so angry I insist that I drive the car up the drive. I prop Ed against the building wall, race to the car, and drive it as close to Ed as possible. It is not easy, but easier, at least. We drive home in silence! Why, why is this harder than it already is?

At home, Ed insists he wants to go to court the next day to see his friend inaugurated as a judge. Ed decides that Lita can take the day off school to help him get there. Weighing up the pros and cons of the situation I'm not happy with this, but it seems so important to Ed that I arrange and book a taxi for an earlier time than necessary. I am hoping that any delays should not hinder them getting to court on time.

Thursday

Lita is happy to stay home from school, of course. I explain the whole situation to her so that she understands the sequence of events. Lita cannot get Ed in and out of the wheelchair herself, even though she knows the drill; she is just too small. Someone has promised to look out for Ed and Lita outside the court rooms to assist Lita get Ed into the wheelchair.

I leave for work feeling reasonably satisfied that all is arranged. Not long after starting work, Lita rings me to say the taxi hasn't arrived; it is well overdue and Ed has become agitated and angry that there is no transport. I have to apologise to the patient I am attending to, leave the consultation and ring the taxi company to see what the delay is. It seems that it has been a very busy morning and I get the impression that no one is fussed that no taxi has been available. Eventually, I am able to arrange for another taxi to be at our place by nine thirty AM. I ring and let Lita know what I have arranged, but now I am concerned that there is no guarantee that the person waiting outside the court rooms will still be there when they arrive. I feel the extreme pressure of the situation but am quite impotent about the outcome. What more can I do? I have to pull myself together and resume working. I am now well behind my appointment schedule.

Friday

Friday already. Didn't sleep well last night. Must get up. I need to meditate. Need to clear my frustration, then a lot to do. Sebi is coming home today. I can't wait. I hope he's had a good time.

After eight AM, we leave the house, but the carer rostered for this morning hasn't arrived yet. Should be here any moment. Ed says he can hang on and wait in bed. In the car. I ring the agency to see if the carer is on our roster and that there are no problems. The agency informs me that the carer won't be in this morning! Oh hang on. It's 8:15, and it's only because I have rung that you now tell me no one is coming to attend to Ed. This is just not okay. How can you do this to us? How can you do this to a person lying in bed incapacitated? This is someone who cannot help himself at all! I have a raging argument, with Lita listening. She has heard all this before, it's nothing new, but she still cringes every time this happens. A drama within an unfolding drama. Lita and Sebi find this all overwhelming.

Eventually, I am able to impress on the manager how critical this is and, reluctantly, she says she will arrange for someone to come over. This is too, too hard.

I do some errands on the way home after dropping off Lita at school and arrive home to find that Ed was not able to hold on till the carer arrived. The carer can only attend to Ed's immediate needs, as he is scheduled to attend another client shortly.

Again I need to ring Terry, our case manager, and see how these rosters can be made more foolproof.

I do some washing, and arrange lunch for Ed and his visitor. As soon as I can after the visitor's arrival, I leave, first to finish my week's shopping and, second, to just be out of the house and be by myself for a while before I pick up the children.

Weekend

Isn't it always the way? Couldn't sleep well, so I get up and meditate. The children don't come into our bedroom anymore except sometimes for a quick good morning. No more rolling in bed, no more tickles, no more fun. All our little spontaneous fun times have gone, flown away surreptitiously as we all just struggle with our daily lives. Ed feels very vulnerable physically and, I am sure, psychologically, as well.

Time to get Ed up and organise him for the day. We are going to my parents for dinner in the evening. It's a change, but everyone is subdued, suppressed. Not that I could expect it to be different.

Drama at my parents. After seating Ed at my parents' dinner table, having said grace, my mother serves Ed's soup in a cup, thinking it will be easier for him, maybe with a straw. I can see Ed is frustrated and can't possibly eat it this way, he says so and this upsets my mother as I understand she has done her best. Everyone is suddenly on edge, the atmosphere is electric.

Silence.

No one knows what to do. There is so much pain, anger, disappointment and none of us has the skills to deal with it all. How do you make a situation such as this real, honest, where everyone is grappling with their own fears and inadequacies? Somehow, the equilibrium is regained and the evening finishes pleasantly. Ed would stay longer, but I am so tired and, knowing what's ahead to get everyone to bed, I want to leave fairly early.

CHAPTER 27

ED'S VISITORS

A man standing tall with a smile on his face,
A man chasing his children as if all in a race.
A man sitting slumped, his mind sharp as ever
Gazing at his children etched in his mind forever.

How to encapsulate a man's life? How to give credit to a life full of hope and despair? How to give credence to the positive sides of a personality that struggled, as we all do, against the tide of life and the emotional baggage that we all carry?

Ed, coming from a strict Catholic background reinforced by a Catholic education, revelled in the freedoms that university life offered him. Ed quickly embraced university life, with all its temptations. Playing cards in a haze of smoke with a cigarette dangling from the corner of his mouth seemed to be an exhilarating way to pass the day and to miss a few lectures, as well. Ed was renowned for his ability to play cards well, but his circle of friends would do battle with him, nonetheless. As a freshman, Ed joined a Latvian fraternity, and it was through this organisation that his closest friendships were established.

It was at this time that I met Ed. He was likeable, friendly, a gentle giant with a ready smile and a peaceful demeanour. Ed displayed an easy-going manner that belied the insecurities that he battled with inside. These he hid well from the outside world, as we all tend to do. Ed could do battle with anyone professionally, for here intellect ruled and emotions were best kept at bay. He could play in most social arenas, for here he portrayed the façade he enjoyed: an engaging man ready to interact with anyone. But within the family he came from, he could never quite match their expectations. He may have had the title of golden boy, but there was always a message of dissatisfaction from his family that he was not fitting the role as expected. There were constant arguments with his mother about his poor approach to his religion and acid recriminations from his sisters about the privileges he was given above them. Close on these repetitive arguments would be their dissatisfactions with me, fabricated out of minds that felt insecure in their own lives. Ed would argue with each and every member of his family but, in the end, would concede that his continuing relationship with them was more important than walking away from them. Ed's loyalty to his family was paramount above all. This had sad repercussions within our own relationship, which floundered as a result.

With his children, he could be himself, from fun loving to wise to interactive to worldly. He was accepted for who he was, unconditionally. There were no disputes, no recriminations, no undue expectations.

As Ed's illness progressed, rosters had to be organised so he could be fed at the lunchtimes I was not available. Ed enjoyed setting up these rosters and went to great lengths to include everyone who expressed a willingness to feed him. These were colleagues, acquaintances, friends, and family. Each indicated their availability. The roster was then planned by Ed on the computer. Ed would devise a month's roster, print it, and then have it sent to each person.

It was not only the practical aspects of these rosters that mattered, it was the social as well. Each lunchtime would see someone else come to feed Ed. They were all from different walks of life, coming to be with Ed for a short time, as he held court. I would prepare the lunch and leave the instructions on the kitchen bench.

In the beginning of this phase, while Ed's swallowing was still reasonable, he would share some of his wine with a fellow wine connoisseur. With Maris, it was their weekly curry ritual. A few friends would take it upon themselves occasionally to take Ed out to lunch.

Our house was now open house to all. No key was necessary, the door was always unlocked.

These people would dedicate a few hours of their day, once, twice, or a few of them three or four times a month. For some, in the beginning, it was probably not easy. It took a certain courage to come into our home, go through the process of feeding Ed and attempt a staccato conversation. Others, such as Maris, saw it as a privilege to feed their friend and spend a few hours with a man who was fading away.

There were times when I would arrive home to find that the person who should have fed Ed had not turned up. I felt sorry for Ed; I felt sorry for the one who had forgotten. It was so easy to do, when everyone's life seemed to be so busy.

There was a time between October 1997 and February 1998 when Ed's. voice deteriorated so it was very difficult to understand what he was saying. The children and I still managed, as our hearing had adapted to Ed's vocal changes, but even we found it hard at times.

Then along came an acquaintance with a laser pointer attached to glasses and an alphabet board drawn up. By putting on the glasses and moving his head slowly, Ed could spell out what he wanted to say via the board. This apparatus came as a real blessing for everyone concerned, and most of all for Ed, who was desperate to communicate and remain an active participant in any conversation. Moss summed it up well, saying it was a Godsend to again be able to understand what Ed was trying so hard to say.

When Maris saw this board, he immediately took it upon himself to make up a professional alphabet board with each relevant alphabet letter square diagonally divided to cater for conversing both in Latvian and English. Instead of using the glasses, the laser pointer was sewn onto one of Sebi's many caps. A foot switch was devised so Ed could switch the laser beam on and off according to his needs.

From this point, conversation again became relatively easy, although slow. Everyone was relieved, for now each visitor no longer had to guess what Ed was saying. This board took some of the frustration out of Ed's life, which now became very busy.

First came the morning carer, who, before leaving, would set Ed up at his computer. Following the carer, there could be someone from the hospital Ed attended infrequently. Maybe it would be the occupational therapist, to see how Ed was doing with his swallowing and to organise the necessary changes to his computer so that he could keep using it. Or it could be the physiotherapist from the hospital to see how Ed was coping and to inform us on the progress of organising an electric wheelchair for Ed. Or it could be the doctor from Monash researching motor neuron disease. He wanted first-hand contact with MND people to add the human dimension to his research.

There were a number of occasions when the visiting hospital staff would tactfully express their impression of Ed. Ed had definite ideas on how he wanted certain things to happen. The awaited wheelchair was a good example of this.

The order for the electric wheelchair had been placed well before necessary, as the requirements were very individualized. This wheelchair needed to be operated by Ed's knee, as his hands were now incapable of any movement at all. I never thought it would be of any value for Ed's situation, but he insisted, feeling it would give him a freedom he did not have, as he could not move from the computer to the recliner without assistance. He felt this wheelchair would give him that independence. It was not possible, as all Ed's movements had to be assisted due to his inability to use his arms or legs at all, and his body generally.

It was during this time that there was an occasion when the physiotherapist from the hospital rang to see how Ed was doing and to tell me the latest on the manufacture of this wheelchair. Her opening remark to me was, "How is Ed, and is he 'jogging along okay?'" How could anyone in her position be so seemingly insensitive and tactless by enquiring in such a manner? I had become confident enough not to allow such remarks to pass without comment. I also commented that, as the wheelchair was taking so long to make, I felt it would not be suitable for Ed's needs. To this, she replied that it was worthwhile and it was what Ed wanted. Maybe Ed's wants were not always what needed to be satisfied. Maybe some sense should prevail. After this, I stepped back from this situation as well, for I could see that my comments were falling on deaf ears all round.

The day would continue, with Ed being visited by the pastoral worker of the hospice, a volunteer to change Ed's library books, Terry, the hospice doctor, a Reiki therapist, or Aldis. There was a constant stream of people to attend to Ed's needs, wants, requests, band, sometimes, demands.

I was pleased to see that under the circumstances Ed's life was full, rich in diversity, and tailored to his needs. Certainly physically, he was totally restricted, but intellectually, his life was abundant.

ALLELUIA!

When my time is near to die and you should hear of it,
come often
and stay with me a while to visit,
for I will be lonely and will need to be close to
people. Look at me and talk about dying
without "watching your words,"
for it will leave me free to tell you if I'm
frightened. Tell me if you love me,
for it will comfort and give me courage to go-
and if we cry together,
I thank you for sharing your grief in leaving the world,
for I don't want to leave it.
But when it's done, let your grief be finished-
and give praise to him who died that we might live,
for in death I jump head-long and straight-way
into eternity,
right into the beginning of the rest of my life!
Alleluia!

-Author unknown.

CHAPTER 28

―――――― ✻ ――――――

ED'S JOURNEY

How do I struggle to hold my own,
So easy to project
To express what I want.
But deep inside I manage to frown
At the turbulence that bubbles from below.
The strength that escapes me
To let go of past pain
To find and honour my soul once again.

Flashes of a fading life: angry, exasperating, exhausting. A myriad of images: sad, longing, heart wrenching, and incredulous. All etched in my mind, no thought of escape.

Life kept dealing out the lessons, one by one, sometimes not so gently and ever persistently.

We visited the hospital neurologist mostly as a formality, but also so the next phase of help could be put into place. If the neurologist happened to walk past us in the car park as I was struggling to get Ed out of the car, there would be no flicker of recognition. In her hospital rooms, her face remained bereft of emotion. She left the kindly conversation to her assistant! There was no interaction; she was just a reserved professional doing her job. But, again, Ed was not prepared to confront her, not prepared to challenge her attitude.

A few weeks prior to Ed's death, his breathing became so shallow that it caused him to panic one morning, as he was being attended to by the carer. The morning carer then panicked and called me on my mobile as I was taking the children to school. We had stopped at a café so I could buy the children each a morning treat. I was in the middle of this busy café, trying to juggle money, two children, a waiter waiting for his money, and listening to my phone instructions. On hearing the carer's dilemma, I suddenly became calm and focused. I gave instructions to the carer and then immediately rang and left a message with the hospice doctor to call me. By the time I arrived home, Ed had calmed down. The hospice doctor rang to say she had relayed instructions to our local GP, Dr Z, and I could go and pick up the script for morphine. On arrival, Dr Z, whom I had not seen for well over twelve months, greeted me in the reception area of his rooms. He immediately spurted forth on the dangers of morphine, stating that government approval was necessary if it was to be used for a lengthy period of time. I was flabbergasted. There was no enquiry as to how Ed was doing, and no empathetic enquiry how the family was doing, just the cold practicalities of the medication and its administration. It was such a hurtful rebuff, so callous in the circumstances. I came out reeling with disbelief. Yet again it seemed that fear reigned and Dr. Z's reaction, I assume, was a direct result of this.

Ed's father came for a visit while he was in Australia on holidays. He was still looking for a fight, still needing to make a stand against me, my parents, and our way of life. When does such anger subside, when does it find a resting place? It certainly did not when he observed his emaciated son. Ed, at least in this instance, had the temerity to throw him out verbally.

Ed's mother, on another occasion, complained about her painful arthritis. Here was a woman in her sixties, who had struggled to raise her own family, seen her children establish their own lives, and then watched how each contended with their own challenges. Though at times she could display acts of kindness, her life had moulded her into a harsh woman focused on herself and her narrow beliefs. There were also many old people that I came into contact with who stated they were old, and lamented about what they could expect of themselves and life, or voiced rhetorically that they really had nothing to complain about, but still they expected a sympathetic ear. All these people seemed to be jesting with life, dishonouring the wealth of their life, when here was a man of forty-eight, in the last stages of his life, half lived, half fulfilled.

We continued to take Ed out to the cinema or for a walk along the beach, with wheelchair, seat cushion, headrest, head cushions, and neck brace. The children knew the routine off by heart. All would be piled into the station wagon, Ed made as comfortable as possible, and off we would go. I became an expert at which cinemas we could depend on for reliable wheelchair access, and infuriated if wheelchair parking spots were occupied by cars without a wheelchair sticker. So we would have a family outing, of sorts, just to take us out of our reality, even partially.

The choking episodes became more prevalent as Ed's throat muscles continued to deteriorate. We would be out with friends for a meal, everyone sitting around chatting and enjoying the meal, the children racing around with their friends. Then suddenly, while being fed, Ed would succumb to an acute choking fit. The food would become lodged in the slack muscles of his throat and his body would reflexively attempt to bring it up again. There were times when he struggled for half an hour to clear the food in his throat. I would wipe the sputum as he continued to struggle to bring up the food. I would break out in a cold sweat, feeling vulnerable, exposed, alienated, while doing my best to deal with this. Someone would come up later and whisper in Ed's ear that they admired his courage. Was it courage he was displaying, or persistence, or an unrelenting attitude to an illness with no let-up?

Until the last few months, Ed was still hoping for a miracle. Yes, we both believed in miracles, but Ed's conviction had long waned. Since Christmas 1997, after exploring for the first time the Amyotrophic Lateral Sclerosis internet site, he had conversed on the computer with a man in Goulburn who had put together a natural therapy programme that he claimed had kept his MND symptoms at bay. Why had it taken Ed so long to look at this site? Why had he left it so late to explore this avenue? This man, whom we met, had a passion. He was, it struck me, pursuing his vision. He was following a logical path that impressed Ed. Ed could have done all this and more; his scientific background would have been of enormous help. But he never did this, though for six months he went through the ritual of following this man's suggested regime.

Were these the last vestiges of fear that Ed was displaying: fear that he hadn't explored every avenue, fear that he had let his family down, fear that he was coming close to dying, fear of unfinished business?

This man who displayed such conviction in God and the afterlife was still displaying the human frailties that we all battle with, such as worrying about a small skin cancer on his forehead and thinking this might bring an end to his life instead of MND. It was through this saga that I realised just how much fear Ed still harboured and how many unresolved issues were still buried within him. I attempted a number of times to talk him through these fears so he could appreciate the perspective he was adhering to, but to no avail. It was only after enlisting the help of Moss and the hospice doctor that Ed was able to understand what was happening to him and to relinquish some of this fear.

The frustrations were many for all four of us. Ed would tap his foot on the floor to get our attention. I would come running from wherever I was in the house to see what he needed. Sometimes, Ed would have been tapping his foot for quite a while to get my attention, as I would have been at the other end of the house and not hear. He would be frustrated that no one had heard him, and I would be frustrated, too, as I had been snatching a moment to do something. Ed might have slid in his chair and need to be rearranged, or perhaps he required the bathroom. I would go through the ritual with the alphabet board to learn what his request was, or I would try to guess. These were terrible times, all of us caught in our own worlds struggling to meet each others needs and many times failing abysmally.

Ed's foot tapping became his means of getting someone's attention. He would tap his foot to indicate to Lita that she was not playing her flute correctly during a practice session in front of him. Or, Ed would tap his foot to draw Sebi's attention to something he wanted changed on the computer. Here, Sebi's anger became evident, as a tussle of wills would ensue. Ed wanted Sebi's undivided attention and full acceptance of his needs on the computer. But Sebi wanted to display his knowledge and to receive his father's approval. Ed would become angry with Sebi, who would eventually be reduced to tears. Here was an eleven-year-old boy grappling with his father's illness and wanting recognition for his efforts of helping his papa, when all he really wanted to do was run away from the man he felt was slowly abandoning him.

On the other hand, Lita could be seen sitting on the armchair of Ed's recliner, hands draped around her papa, cradling his head, relishing the moment, absorbing into her being the very essence of this short relationship.

They were two souls crying out for reprieve as they best knew how, one hanging on to her papa the same way she clung to her pain, the other trying to extricate himself from an ever engulfing pain that he could not allow to control him for fear of a total breakdown.

With ever more frequency, it took sheer willpower to keep going, to keep my exasperations and mounting fatigue at bay. Nights were the worst, starting with arranging Ed in bed for the night. He would need to be placed on his right side, top leg bent more than the right, resting on the bed. His arms and hands were like cumbersome, non-pliant appendages that needed to be positioned, supported by pillows, so he could feel comfortable and his position would not interfere with his breathing. This was the hardest. With no alphabet board to guide us, the carer and I would struggle to arrange Ed's body to his liking. This could take fifteen minutes of guesswork and rearranging. Some nights, I would be woken up five or six times by Ed muttering a need for change, I would do my best but, woken from a momentary deep sleep or having just fallen asleep, it was exhausting and debilitating. Many times, I was reduced to tears by the sheer unrelenting wave of demands made upon me. There was no one to really share this with who could or would understand.

All this would fade for a moment when Ed would relate one of his encounters with his sisters. Apart from the continual criticisms of me, the worst episode surely was when his eldest sister decided to bring their retarded sibling for a visit, without Ed's consent. Ed was subjected to a situation he could no longer handle. By now, unable to cry or laugh in an uninhibited way due to fear of not being able to breath, Ed had a restricted ability to physically express himself. Ed's laughs were huge smiles, his tears an upturned lip with moist eyes. Here was a time, though, that Ed did allow his anger to show and impress on his sister her insensitivity.

Ed's fragile physical state allowed limited emotional outlet, and this was most poignantly lived by all four of us on Ed's last Father's Day. A numbness had pervaded me for some time: no more tears, no more hopes, no more. Yet on Father's Day morning, two little souls honoured their father with their love. They hopped into bed as was our custom, to greet their papa on his day, to show them their presents for him. A little girl with a book made at school about her father, not about things they were enjoying together, but of memories past and gone. A boy patting his papa's hand and handing him his handmade card of thanks. Through the silent numbness, the tears still rose; I was humbled by the honesty in all its rawness. The pain was so acute, our situation so overwhelming, that even raw emotions could no longer be expressed. There was just this paralysis.

In contrast, how different this was from Ed's last birthday a few days later, that seemed to both of us such a farce of justifications, excuses, and convention.

There were some who came with their cards, their flowers, and their embraces. There were others who gave reasons for not visiting Ed over the past nine months, and others who were embarrassed at not knowing he could no longer drink wine, yet presented him with a bottle of wine. Still others came with a stream of excuses perhaps, blind to how inappropriate their gifts were. Yet they came, as if by doing so they would be abdicated of their insecure behaviour.

How sad that only a few came with a thank you in their hearts to honour the man and to celebrate his short life.

CHAPTER 29

———— ❦ ————

HEAVEN BOUND

May the trail that I leave
As I travel through time
Allow the light that I see
Help me discover my soul.

Ed was desperately watching the wall clock in his hospice room as he lay in bed, watching as the minute hand kept ticking past five o'clock. Where was his family, when would they arrive?

Ed had had a terrible day. Nothing seemed right; he didn't know what he wanted. Pat was his lunchtime visitor. Pat suggested each of the soups I had pre-prepared, but on this day, none were to Ed's liking. He eventually settled on a breakfast menu.

After Pat's visit, Ed was put to bed and a butterfly attachment placed in his abdomen for easy morphine administration. His breathing had suddenly become quite laboured, and the morphine helped to reduce the stress with easy dosage availability.

Ed was restless and dissatisfied all day. Where was the peace that should have been his? Was he aware of the journey he was about to embark upon, the one he and I had discussed so many times? Was he aware that he was about to leave us and wanting to see us one more time?

I had promised him that I would be there, when the time came, to help him cross over to the other side. I so hoped to make the transition easier for him, or so I thought. God knew better! God knew how hard it would have been for Ed to see his family one last time as he was leaving.

While we were travelling to the hospice, God in His infinite wisdom gently took Ed away.

Suddenly, we were catapulted into a new journey. It was the three of us, not four; it was I, not we. We were living now what we had known would be.

We arrived, as we always did, at the ambulance entrance. Somewhere in the background, staff were murmuring that Ed's condition suddenly turned for the worst. This was so unexpected. But, what did it matter! I was not there as I promised! What a foolish promise!

Sebi, Lita, and I entered Ed's room in silence, as if in a tomb. There he lay, in the darkened room, his cap covering his folded hands across his chest. Here was the skeleton of the man who once was a testimony of a man who had fought and struggled through the tougher walks of life. Wait, where was this man whose life was over in a flash? Where did it go so quickly?

We stayed to honour and caress the man, something which, in life, we had found so hard to do. We prayed, we hugged, we cried, until Maris arrived. I had rung Maris on the way to the hospice. Here he was again, when needed. He took the children to get them some dinner just as Graham was arriving. No reason. Graham just had the urge to visit his friend.

Some time later, the staff came in to see if we would like to help wash Ed and change his clothes. The staff and I washed Ed's emaciated body for the last time, and dressed him in some fresh clothes.

We stayed until well after ten o'clock. The children were exhausted; it was time to say goodbye.

There we stood, saying our farewells to the man who had been so many things to us all; for me, spanning over thirty years.

Edgar, thank you for being my teacher. I was such a poor pupil at times. Thank you, not just for the good times, but for the painful ones as well. May you continue to travel and learn to cherish your essence on your journey to heaven.

www.ingramcontent.com/pod-product-compliance
Lightning Source LLC
Chambersburg PA
CBHW021638120626
46545CB00002B/599